Creating Positive Personal Images for Professional Success

Second Edition

Patsy Johnson Hallman

Rowman & Littlefield Education

A division of
ROWMAN & LITTLEFIELD PUBLISHERS, INC.
Lanham • New York • Toronto • Plymouth, UK

Published by Rowman & Littlefield Education
A division of Rowman & Littlefield Publishers, Inc.
A wholly owned subsidiary of
The Rowman & Littlefield Publishing Group, Inc.
4501 Forbes Boulevard, Suite 200, Lanham, Maryland 20706
www.rowman.com

10 Thornbury Road, Plymouth PL6 7PP, United Kingdom

Copyright © 2012 by Patsy Johnson Hallman

All rights reserved. No part of this book may be reproduced in any form or by any electronic or mechanical means, including information storage and retrieval systems, without written permission from the publisher, except by a reviewer who may quote passages in a review.

British Library Cataloguing in Publication Information Available

Library of Congress Cataloging-in-Publication Data

Hallman, Patsy Johnson, 1935–
  Creating positive personal images for professional success / Patsy Johnson Hallman.
    p. cm.
  Rev. ed. of: Creating positive images : a guide for young people. c2004.
  Includes bibliographical references.
  ISBN 978-1-61048-776-4 (cloth : alk. paper) — ISBN 978-1-61048-777-1 (pbk. : alk. paper) — ISBN 978-1-61048-778-8 (electronic)
  1. Etiquette for young adults. 2. Self-presentation. I. Hallman, Patsy Johnson, 1935– Creating positive images II. Title.
  BJ1857.Y58H35 2012
  650.1—dc23   2012014262

∞^{TM} The paper used in this publication meets the minimum requirements of American National Standard for Information Sciences—Permanence of Paper for Printed Library Materials, ANSI/NISO Z39.48-1992.

Printed in the United States of America

This book is dedicated to my grandchildren.

Contents

Preface ... vii

Acknowledgments ... ix

Part I: Positive Personal Image

1 Projecting a Positive Personal Image ... 3
2 Creating a Positive Image with Clothing ... 9
3 A Positive Image in Public Places ... 19
4 Travel Etiquette ... 27
5 At the Table ... 31
6 As a Visitor ... 39

Part II: Effective Communication

7 Introductions and Titles ... 45
8 Practical Guidelines for Effective Communication ... 51
9 Communicating with Social Media ... 61

Part III: Relationships

10 Guidelines for Relating to Others in a Positive Manner ... 67
11 Responding to People Who Are Experiencing Major Life Events ... 75

Part IV: Professionalism

12	Interview Skills	83
13	The Professional at Work	89
14	Selected Professional Responsibilities	95
15	Social Responsibilities at Work	99
16	Growing Professionally	103

References	109
About the Author	111

Preface

This book is written for professional people who seek success, whether they are new professionals or experienced ones seeking higher-level positions. Successful people use various resources to reach their personal and professional goals. Among such resources are the guidelines found in the units of this book. Topics are grouped into four units: Positive Personal Image, Effective Communication, Relationships, and Professionalism.

A profession is made up of workers who have specialized knowledge and skills. Professional people are found in medicine, law, education, finance, and many other fields that have specific characteristics. Those specific characteristics are a *unique knowledge base that was acquired through special education and training, a service orientation* (as opposed to the profit motive), adherence to a *code of ethics*, and an *organization for self-governing and entrance into the profession.*

The knowledge and skills base, for most professions, requires long-term studies, as in preparation for medicine. The *service orientation*, as priority, may be seen clearly in education. For example, effective teachers show strong loyalty to their students, parents, and school district. While all have a *code of ethics*, probably none is more well-known that that of medicine. Ethics go beyond legal consideration to decisions made on the basis of needs of the client. The value of *organizational structures* to professions is that it provides a vehicle for the members to govern themselves.

Acknowledgments

I am grateful to the many experts in the fields of professionalism, ethics, relationships, education, communication, and etiquette who have provided sources for my knowledge in the area of professional success. People at all levels, from university students to experienced business professionals, have inspired me to continue to work in this area as a means of service for individuals and groups. Through the years, students of all ages have enriched my professional life. I am especially grateful for those at Stephen F. Austin State University.

My husband, Dr. Leon Hallman, has been a supporter and advisor throughout the process of creating this book for young professionals. My children, Dave Lyndon Spurrier and Bethany Spurrier, who are managers in large organizations, were especially helpful in the area of social media. Michael Spurrier gave excellent input on the chapter about sportsmanship and good manners for athletes. Mr. Nick Shelton, art teacher at Nacogdoches High School, shared his talent in creating the illustrations.

Tom Koerner, Mary McMenamin, and Karen Ackermann, with Rowman & Littlefield, have been helpful, gracious, and cooperative throughout the development of this manuscript, which is a second edition of one of their earlier publications, *Creating Positive Self-Images for Young People*. I am grateful to them for every suggestion and every discussion we have had as the additions and changes were made.

PART I

POSITIVE PERSONAL IMAGE

CHAPTER 1

Projecting a Positive Personal Image

In this chapter:

1. the importance of a positive self-image
2. ways to project self-confidence
3. how to get the responses you want from others
4. selected skills for reaching your personal goals
5. introducing yourself
6. remembering names

Creating a positive self-image is important for at least three good reasons. First, knowing how to conduct yourself in the best possible manner gives you *confidence.* With confidence, you are more comfortable, and life is more satisfying than when you are lacking in confidence. Second, when people project a positive self-image they are more likely *to get the response they want* from other people, because, in general, people respond positively if they are approached positively. And, third, with a positive attitude, you are more likely to be *productive*; that is, you are more likely to reach your own personal and professional goals.

The information in this book will help you build a positive image, which is a valuable tool for achieving professional success. As a new professional, or as a professional person who is moving up the career ladder, the information will be useful. Read about how you may present yourself in a positive manner. Then continue with considering ways to interact successfully with people in a wide range of social and professional situations. Consider these comments from young adults who were asked about the importance of a positive self image.

Michael: "I feel free to enter into my professional role when I know that I look like a professional person."

Katherine: "I want to be able to talk with anyone about whatever topic is under discussion. If I am confident about grammar, information, and tactful discussion, I know I can do that."

Ali: "I feel confident when I can meet other professional people with ease; when I can act in ways that result in positive responses."

PRESENTING YOURSELF

When you meet someone for the first time, the person you meet forms an opinion of you in the first thirty seconds of your encounter. That first opinion is so strong that it takes many successive visits to change the first impression you created. If you want to make positive impressions (i.e., if you want people to admire you) there are specific things you can do in order to get positive responses.

What to Do for a Positive Response

Three factors affect the first impression you make: first, your posture and body movements, second, how you dress and groom yourself, and third, what you say. For example, imagine a teacher walking through a hallway of a school building slumped over and looking at the floor as he walks. Now, contrast that look with one you get from a man who walks purposefully down the hallway, head up, eyes alert, speaking to students and colleagues he meets. Those two examples create very different impressions, don't they? That is because posture and the way you carry your body tell others either that you are confident, mature, and successful, or that you are sad, shy, and uncomfortable with yourself.

Introducing Yourself

It is all right, in fact, it is often important for you to introduce yourself. Do so with a greeting and with your full name. "Good morning, I'm Keith Burns." Pronounce your name slowly and distinctly.

Many people say their first name clearly but they slur their last name, saying "I am Patricia Hal . . . (mumble)," rather than "I am Patricia Hallman." A careful person places as much emphasis on pronouncing her last name as clearly as her first name.

As a younger person, you often said, when you met other young people, "Hi, I'm Keith," but in the adult world, confident and mature people use full names. Always give your first and last name when introducing yourself to adults. When you introduce yourself to children and youth, use the title you expect them to use when they speak to you. For example, if you are the school principal, introduce yourself to students as "Mr. Burns, your principal."

Eye Contact and Hand Shakes

Look eye to eye at the person you are meeting. When people encounter others, they show signs of strong character in two ways. One is with eye contact and the other one is with a strong handshake.

In *social settings*, men always shake hands when they meet, but they shake hands with a woman only if she offers her hand. However, in business settings, both men and women shake hands without regard for gender. Offer your hand with confidence—thumb joint to thumb joint—then give one firm shake.

Some men mistakenly think they should shake just a woman's fingers. Rather, shake hands with a woman just as you do with a man. Of course it is important to avoid a hand squeeze that is so strong that rings cut into fingers.

As you shake hands, look into the person's eyes and speak a greeting. Say something like: "Hello, I'm Sue Smith," or "How do you do?" or "I am so pleased to meet you, Mr. Jones."

When you meet a new person, repeat the name. That serves two purposes. First, it helps you remember the name, and second, it honors the person you are meeting. People of all ages like to hear their own names spoken.

The Power of a Name

There is power in a person's name. Think about that; people like to hear their names called out as ones who has done something well; they enjoy seeing their names (in a complimentary way) in the paper; and they especially like to be referred to in a group by their real names, rather than as "you." *And, they want you to use the name they prefer.*

Here are some comments from people that illustrate those ideas:

> From Scott: I feel especially pleased at school when I see the principal in the cafeteria and she says, "Hello, Scott."

> From Maggie: I know teachers don't have a high opinion of students who have not bothered to remember their teachers' names.

> From Michael's grandmother: I was so proud when we saw one of my older friends at the concert last evening and Michael said, "Hello, Mrs. Cole."

Some people, especially those in roles where they relate to many people, adopt a habit of using a pet name for older people. Right away, the older person suspects that the speaker does not remember his or her name. Statements such as these illustrate that annoying habit:

> "Sweetie, this dress may be just right for you."
> "You old dear, I know you are ready for a good meal."
> "Ralph, is your lovely lady with you?"

Remembering Names

Because names are so powerful, it is important to remember as many as possible. Train yourself in the following steps to remember names of the people you meet.

1. Repeat the name as a part of your response to the introduction: "I am so pleased to meet you, Mrs. Hall."
2. In your mind, associate the person with someone or something you know well: (thinking silently) "Aw, like the hall in a house."
3. As soon as you have the opportunity, write the person's name on a notepad you may have in your pocket or handbag.

4. Repeat the name when you take leave of the person: "Mrs. Hall, I surely enjoyed learning about the new company that you will be representing in our town."

REMEMBER:

You choose whether to show the world that you are either a positive, confident person or a negative person by the way you speak to others, by the way you walk and act, and by the way you dress and groom yourself.

CHAPTER 2

Creating a Positive Image with Clothing

In this chapter:

1. the importance of clothing and grooming
2. professional dress
3. how style may be used to create the look you desire
4. how to choose colors to compliment skin tones
5. the impact of appropriate clothing for specific occasions

CLOTHING AND FIRST IMPRESSIONS

The clothing you wear defines your personal image more than any other factor in your appearance. Clothing choices speak for the wearer. They say "concerned with appearance" or "little or no concern for appearance." Clothing may say "neat" or "sloppy." Or it may speak to style, as "old-fashioned" or "trendy" or "classic" or "fashionable."

Many times clothing also communicates roles we fill. With little thought, we think "nurse" when we see a woman in a white uniform, or "athlete" when we see a man in baseball uniform. A woman dressed in a suit and carrying a briefcase says "business leader," and so it is with other occupations and roles. These clothing messages not only identify a worker but also give the client confidence that the worker is competent. For example, how would you feel if the person who came to your hospital room to give you a shot wore clothing more appropriate for a custodian than for a nurse? Chances are you would question the procedure before allowing it to take place!

Making considered choices about what to wear every time you dress pays off in several ways. First, you feel more confident when you are appropriately dressed; and second, you are more likely to get the responses you want from others when you are dressed appropriately. Finally, you show respect and consideration for people and events by what you wear.

Think of how carefully you planned at some point in time when you were called on to make a public presentation. If you plan that carefully every day you will always be well-dressed and appropriately dressed for every occasion.

People show respect, or lack of it, by their clothing choices. For example, for a funeral, considerate people wear modest, subtle-colored clothing suitable for church or other similar occasions. In this way they acknowledge the seriousness of the occasion and they show respect for the family of grievers.

CHOOSING YOUR WARDROBE

Ask yourself, "What image do I want to create?" Your answer will determine what clothing you buy and how you dress yourself. Perhaps you will answer with one of these:

- the professional look
- the independent, free-spirit look
- the classic look
- a western look
- a conservative look
- a sexy look

APPROPRIATE DRESS

Several practices help you make choices about your total wardrobe and about dress for work and for special occasions. One of them is preparing for buying before you begin shopping. Here are ways to prepare for making the best choices.

- Observe what successful people in your profession wear.
- Assess your body shape as well as your personal preference.
- When you are concerned about appropriateness for a special occasion, ask the person who invited you to an event what is appropriate dress.
- Read magazines that feature social and work sections, looking at pictures that illustrate dress.
- Talk to knowledgeable clothing salespeople as you make selections.

CLOTHES FOR YOUR UNIQUE BODY FEATURES

Your body size and shape should dictate many choices you make about clothing. For example, if you are very short, and you want to look taller, you should choose tops and bottoms of the same color. On the other hand, if you want to look shorter, choose contrasting colors for tops and bottoms. Here are some guidelines for creating a body image with clothing.

Table 2.1.

If you want to look:	Wear:
shorter	contrasting tops and bottoms horizontal lines
taller	same color tops and bottoms vertical lines
slimmer	darker colors tailored clothing v-neck shirts or blouses
heavier	bright color fuller, looser garments
less hippy	dark bottoms, bright tops

USE COLOR TO CREATE IMAGES

Color can be used as a tool to create personal image. Think of someone who is considered to be an energetic, vivacious lady. She probably wears a lot of color—lots of reds perhaps. In other words, the colors that such a person chooses to wear emphasize the image of a youthful, energetic person. Other colors carry images as well. For example, blue is calming, green is soothing, brown is somber, white typifies purity, and black projects solemnity. People who wear black to a funeral use color for the image they want to project at that specific event. Research shows that blue is the color to wear when you are concerned about being accepted by a group. People often (conscientiously or unconscientiously) choose to wear gray or brown when they are feeling sad or depressed.

While it is true that colors communicate feelings and may also communicate signs of respect, color can also be powerful as a compliment to individual skin tones. Colors that are in harmony with your skin coloring enhance your natural good looks.

Color and Skin Tone

All human skin has either a bluish or a goldish tone. This is true for both men and women, for both young and old people, and for people of all skin colors. Look at the skin on the inside of your wrist. Can you tell if your skin is bluish or golden? It is easy to determine your skin tones if you hold your wrist close to the wrists of two other people and see the differences. When you do determine which of the two tones is dominant in your skin, you can begin to choose colors in clothing to compliment your natural coloring.

People with bluish skin tones wear cool colors well. These include:

- black
- white
- blue
- green
- purple
- lavender
- rose
- wine
- fuchsia
- nautical colors
- pure red
- icy colors

People with golden skin tones wear warm colors well. These include:

- yellow
- orange
- coral pink
- orange-red
- brown
- off-white

CLOTHING FOR SUCCESS

The well-dressed person is not necessarily the person with the most clothes. Rather, the well-dressed person is the person who dresses his best or her best every day. That is, the person gives attention to clothing every day. Regardless of how many clothing items are in your closet or chest, you can only wear one set at a time. Concentrate on making the set of clothing you choose each day one that is right for you and for your activities on that day. Ask yourself these questions:

- Am I well-groomed?
- Have I used cosmetics appropriately?
- Are my clothes clean and free of wrinkles?
- Do my clothes fit my body properly?
- Do my accessories compliment my clothing?
- Am I wearing clothes in good taste for my responsibilities today?
- Am I dressed appropriately for the occasions I will face today?
- Will I project the image today that I want?
- What will others think of my appearance today?
- Will my appearance help me reach my goals today?
- Will my appearance reflect maturity or immaturity, confidence or lack of self-confidence?

GROOMING FOR A POSITIVE IMAGE

The first essential for creating a pleasing personal appearance is good grooming. A clean body, clean hair in a neat, current style, and nails that are neat and clean are essential for getting a positive response from others.

People who do not practice normal habits of good hygiene have already missed the goal of projecting a positive image. Attention to cleanliness and deodorants are essential. Clean, well-manicured nails and hair in a contemporary style all communicate a positive image. For men who wear facial hair, a neat trim is essential for an everyday good appearance. Some people need the help of a dermatologist to combat normal skin lesions. Dental care, too, is necessary to keep an attractive smile.

Many women find the help of a make-up specialist, one who is trained in selection and application of make-up, important to their getting the appearance they want.

A contemporary hairstyle, one that is right for your own face shape, is critical for good looks. Observe other people your age whose hair you admire. Ask who cut their hair as a way of choosing your own stylist. When you visit the hair stylist, take along a picture of the style you want. Another way to get just the right style is to select a salon that has computer technology that allows you to see how a different style looks on you. Do this before cutting begins. This provides a person with confidence when changing hairstyles.

PROFESSIONAL DRESS

Almost every occupation, and certainly every profession, has a general expectation for dress of employees. For example, while the dress codes or expectations for teachers have relaxed in recent years, it is still important for teachers to dress in ways that produce respect from students and confidence from parents and principals.

A recent survey on dress for teachers (conducted among Texas teachers by Drs. Janie Kenner and Rachel Underwood) showed that expectations varied for men and for women. For women, a jacket, or perhaps a vest, over skirts or pants gave a more professional look than women who wore only a shirt or blouse with pants. For male teachers, a tie with shirt and khaki pants presented the most favored professional look. For both male and female *administrators*, a jacket, was needed to complete the professional look.

With the exception of clothing for physical education teachers, the wearing of workout clothing and workout shoes was found to be unacceptable by all the respondents. The findings of the Kenner/Underwood research clearly showed that students have more respect for teachers who are professionally dressed than for those who are not. The research also showed that discipline was better when the appearance of the teacher was professional. Further, principals were more apt to view the teachers as competent and worthy of promotion if they dressed professionally.

DRESS CODES

Of course, personal likes and dislikes strongly influence a person's choices in clothing and grooming. However, dress and grooming codes of various organizations provide powerful influences on one's choices. For example, many high schools have dress codes for students and teachers. Similarly, many business organizations—banks, accounting firms, etc.—have dress codes for employees. Learn about these required codes before making choices of clothing you will wear in your work environment. Some organizations may say they have no dress codes; however, you will probably find that they have very strong "expectations" for the dress of their employees. Observe what others who are successful in the organization wear. Chances are great that what those successful people wear represents the prevailing dress code—written or not.

BALANCING PERSONAL LIKES AND DISLIKES WITH PUBLIC EXPECTATIONS

Many people have conflicting values that enter into their clothing and grooming choices. If that is the case for you, use the same decision-making process for deciding on clothing and grooming as you do in making other types of choices. You probably remember that these are the steps to successful decision making.

- Identify the problem
  - Consider all the options
  - Anticipate the outcome of each choice

- Ask yourself these questions about each option:
  - What will others think of my choice?
  - Would I make this choice a second time?
  - How will others respond to this choice?
  - How will I feel about this choice?
  - Will this choice help me reach my next goal?
- Make your choice
- Afterward, evaluate your choice and the outcome of it

In addition to this proven decision-making practice, here are other serious questions for professional people to consider:

- Have I dressed appropriately for the occasion?
- Is my clothing too revealing?
- How will people I see react to body piercing?
- How much body piercing is enough?
- How will my friends and family react to tattoos?
- Are tattoos for me? If I decide at a later time that they are not, how can they be removed?
- Have I been excessive with my accessories?

CARE OF CLOTHING

The care required to keep clothing looking fresh and neat and appropriate is strongly affected by the fabric and style of the garment. For example, will the garment require dry cleaning or is it washable? Read labels to get this information before buying.

A good habit to develop is to hang, fold, or place in the laundry basket the garments you remove when you change clothes. Keep a small personal mending kit for replacing buttons, repairing hems, etc. Sometimes a supply of safety pins and Scotch tape save the day in a dressing emergency. Reread the care labels before washing your clothing and follow directions carefully.

REMEMBER:

1. Dress and grooming make a strong impact on your personal and professional image.

2. Choices in what you wear often affect your success.
3. Regardless of how many clothes you have or do not have, you can present a positive image with careful choices and upkeep of your garments.

CHAPTER 3

A Positive Image in Public Places

In this chapter:

1. how people are perceived in public places
2. taking care of public property
3. presenting yourself positively in public places
4. the positive athlete
5. sportsmanship

Knowing how to manage yourself in public places is important for your own feelings of well-being as well as for the impressions you make on others. A recent survey among university students revealed some interesting attitudes that young adults have toward public behavior. For example, the young men and women said that there are several things that their friends do when they are in public places that make them uncomfortable.

First, the young people said that they feel uncomfortable when their friends are loud and call attention to their group. Illustrations given were excessive volume with mics and radios. Arguments, too, as well as drunken behavior and erratic driving were in their negative list.

Second, the young adults said that they are uncomfortable when their friends are rude to people in service roles. Some service roles cited were waiters in restaurants, custodians at schools, sales people, and flight attendants. People who are professional and have strong character show respect for others. They do not belittle or make fun of people who are different or who are from other parts of the world.

A third behavior that makes for discomfort among people in public places is couples or parents showing strong emotions in public. Here are some common examples of unattractive public behavior:

1. a dating couple arguing loudly
2. a husband putting down his wife when they are guests in someone else's home
3. a wife fussing at her husband at a party
4. a mother slapping her child in the grocery store
5. a father yelling at his child in public
6. a family allowing a baby to cry in church
7. a couple hugging and kissing at a ballgame
8. adults fighting over a Little League ballgame

THE POSITIVE PUBLIC IMAGE

Review these ways to present a positive image of yourself when you are in public places.

1. In general, practice common courtesies.
2. Avoid loud behavior that calls attention to yourself.
3. Be patient and polite to people in service roles (e.g., waiters, salespeople, maids, etc.).
4. Dress and groom yourself appropriately for the occasion.
5. Smoke only in designated smoking areas. If you use smokeless tobacco, be especially careful about spit cups and the places where you choose to use the tobacco—remember that its use is for extremely informal situations.
6. For men, hats and caps are appropriate *outdoor* wear—wearing a cap indoors seldom projects a positive image. For women, costume hats should be removed when they obstruct the view of others in the group.
7. As a driver, follow courtesies as well as skill—never use an auto to express emotions!
8. Avoid displaying strong emotion in public—for example, arguing with your spouse (or special friend), punishing your children, or being intensely affectionate.

9. Take care of public facilities—avoid trashing, cluttering, etc.
10. Always arrive at theaters and concert halls before a performance begins. Never talk or text during a performance and do wait to leave until there is an intermission.
11. Always stand for the playing of the national anthem (if you are walking into a stadium when the music begin, stop and remain still until the anthem is completed). Men remove their hats or caps as a sign of loyalty to the country and respect for the flag.
12. When small children are invited to your home, prepare your home so that the child may be comfortable and play happily while your valuable possessions are safe.
13. Respond to handicapped people in the same way you respond to others—for example, do not raise your voice, stare, or seek to take away their independence. Offer to help when help is needed, but allow them their independence. Treat them like your other friends and acquaintances.
14. When visiting a friend or acquaintance who is hospitalized, make your visit cheerful and brief.
15. In general tip waiters 15 percent of the bill, taxi drivers 15 percent of the fare, and bellmen $0.50 to $1.00 per bag depending on the size of the bag.
16. Graciously open doors for companions—especially superiors, elderly people, and people with heavy loads—as you walk together.
17. Use standard language—check your speech for grammatical errors, excessive slang, colloquial phrases, and inappropriate jokes. Remember that you can talk with anyone about anything if you have tact and correct vocabulary.
18. When a couple is walking in dark areas, over rough terrain, or in dense crowds, it is thoughtful for the man to offer his arm to the woman.
19. When traveling via public vehicles, use only your allotted space for sitting and storing possessions, be gracious to attendants, and offer your seat to the very old, the handicapped, or someone carrying a baby.

ELEVATORS

Good manners in an elevator differ somewhat from general principles of etiquette.

The rule to remember for using an elevator is "first in, last out," or to say it another way, "last in, first out." That rule works in elevators because if a man is standing just inside the door when it opens, and, thinking to be polite, steps backward to let a women out first, he may step on someone or push into a person behind him. Therefore it is correct for the person nearest the elevator door to get off first, followed in order by others on the elevator.

Another thing to remember about elevators is to wait until all who wish to get off the elevator have exited before you get into the elevator.

If you find yourself in the back of a crowded elevator and it stops at your floor, you may correctly say, "Off, please," and people will shift about to let you out. You might also say, "Excuse me; this is my floor."

SPORTSMANSHIP

Sports are a big part of the American world. Whether you are players, professional sportspeople, or simply spectators, it is wise to consider the concept of sportsmanship and how it may impact behaviors and successes. At least three elements are present in sportsmanship. First is *fairness.* That means that each team has equal opportunity to compete to the best of their ability. An example of unfairness is referees showing favoritism to one of the opposing teams. Just as honesty is the number-one quality that people, in general, want from their associates, so do sportspeople want *fairness in their world of sports.*

Another important factor in sportsmanship is *self-control.* This factor is most often seen in the players, but coaches and parents and other supporters sometimes lose control. Lack of self-control often leads to penalties that cause a team to lose a game. It certainly is a characteristic that gives an individual a negative reputation. Many coaches help athletes develop self-control with such philosophies as "it is just a game—win or lose—move on to the next one." Or within a game, lack of self-management may mean a loss of self-confidence when a player has made an error. A strong coach says to such a player, "Move on to the next play; don't dwell on errors; instead, think of how you will execute the next play."

Being a gracious winner or loser is characteristic of sportsmanship. Examples are the handshakes among opposing teams after a game. By contrast, sore losers are not gracious to the winners and they make excuses for why their team lost. They are not willing to take responsibility. A sore loser is not an attractive person nor a positive team member.

A respected sportsman is persistent in maintaining body health and good physical condition as well as consistently working to increase his skills.

Positive and successful sportspeople realize that they represent their organization whether in the community or on the playing field. They strive for a positive image and behaviors.

PROFESSIONALISM FOR ATHLETES

In today's world, athletic events are some of the most-viewed elements in society. With that, of course, comes the prominence of the athletes. From school-age to professional life, they are appraised by the public. How do these prominent people create positive images?

Coaches for athletes say they expect two major characteristics, or behaviors, from individual team members. First, they want ability and individuals who will work to improve that ability. And, second, they want individuals who are "team players." Whether a university athlete or a professional one, protocol and good manners are important for success.

Consider these ideas. Having good manners means following the rules of the game, as well as living the lifestyle that athletes commit to when joining a specific team or sports program. It also means giving attention to interpersonal relationships.

While interpersonal relationships may seem frivolous to a professional athlete, research shows that relationships with coaches, team members, fans, supporters, teachers, professors, and even the press, are critical to an athlete's success. Good interpersonal relationships build your self-confidence and open doors of opportunity.

How does an athlete build positive relationships? To answer that question, reread the sections in this book on relationships, especially read the section on manners in public places, and then consider manners that apply especially to athletes. Some of the important ones are as follows.

Remember that first impressions are created during your first encounter with another individual. Your posture, your grooming, the clothes you are wearing, even the expression on your face influence that first impression, and it is difficult to change. If you feel a need to improve the impression you make on new acquaintances take these actions:

1. Look around at the other people in your field and select the one you admire most—the one you think is most successful. Then observe her dress and manner. Observe others; then make a decision about changes you could make to your advantage. For example, be sure that you are always well-groomed and are wearing the appropriate clothing for the occasion.
2. Shake hands with a firm shake, and make eye contact, when you are introduced to a new person and when you are meeting your opponents at the conclusion of a game. Use name-remembering techniques to remember the person's name. Then when you take leave of the person, repeat her name: "Coach Brown, it's been good to talk with you; good luck on that next game."
3. Be modest about your own accomplishments. Let someone else mention them in group conversation.
4. If yours is a team sport, always give credit to the whole team when you are complimented.
5. Be loyal to your institution, your coach, and other players. When you can no longer do that, it is time to move on.
6. Be generous with your praise of others.
7. Avoid arguing with the coach; follow instructions.
8. Practice good sportsmanship.
9. Check your speaking habits and determine if you need to make some improvements before you are next interviewed about your game. Practice what you may say to specific sports-related questions; consider your grammar; listen to others who speak about sports, and consider adding new phrases and words to your vocabulary. Not only will this activity make you more admired by others, but it will also be valuable in your next interview and it will build your self-confidence.

10. Remember that you always represent your team when you travel as an athlete.
11. Consider members of the opposing team as opponents, not enemies. Be respectful of them as you do your best to win the game. Of course, follow all rules of the game, but do extras, such as helping a fallen player to get up when he falls.
12. By all means, avoid insulting words to the opponents during your games.

REMEMBER:

1. Public places belong to everyone. The mature person always does her part to keep such places clean and free of graffiti and trash.
2. The image you create in public places affects your overall success.
3. Sportsmanship is a reflection of the ethical character of individual players, coaches, and teams.

CHAPTER 4

Travel Etiquette

In this chapter:

1. how to travel comfortably and happily
2. how to show consideration for others as you travel

Americans love to travel. Two factors have a great influence on the satisfaction one feels when traveling. First, and most important, is the attitude the traveler has toward new places and experiences; toward people and things that are different from those encounter in daily life; and toward fellow travelers. Travel experiences are most enjoyable when the traveler welcomes new sights, sounds, tastes, and local customs. One may wonder why a person with a negative attitude toward other countries and customs chooses to travel.

A second factor that affects enjoyment of travel is the behavior of other people you encounter in your travels. Years ago an author coined a phrase "the ugly American" to describe the rude and inconsiderate traveler. "Ugly travelers" make comments like these:

"They call this steak?"
"Why don't they learn to speak English?"
"I can't eat this food!"
"I expect better service than this when I travel!"
"This looks like 'funny money' to me!"

Professional people, who travel as a part of their work, make efforts to be positive about whatever they encounter, always remembering that they represent their company and their country.

CHAPTER 4

TRAVEL ETIQUETTE

To be sure that you not only represent your country positively when you travel but also enjoy the experience for yourself, review the following rules of travel etiquette.

Good Manners When Traveling by Auto

Whether you are the driver or a passenger in the auto, abide by safe driving rules, including speed limits. Avoid expressing your emotions with your car. For example, immature drivers sometimes want to call attention to themselves or to their new car by "burning off" or exceeding the speed limits or by bragging about "what their car can do." Such action does call attention, but in a very negative way. Resist playing music so loud that it interferes with others. Never yell or call out to people in other cars. Not only is that rude, but also in today's world it can result in the violence of road rage. As a good citizen, keep your trash in a receptacle within the car; never throw it out the car window!

Good Manners When Traveling by Bus

Bus manners include using only one seat per person and being respectful of others. The loud and pushy person creates a strong negative image for himself. The person with good manners also avoids littering the bus; instead, they carry their papers, drink cups, etc., to the trash.

When traveling on a loaded bus, young people and men have opportunities to be especially considerate to women carrying babies and to elderly people. Giving these burdened people your seat is a considerate act.

Traveling by Air

In an airplane, the same good manners apply as people observe in bus travel. In addition, it is especially important to show consideration for flight attendants—not demanding too much time, nor being critical, and never flirting with them. Complaining about safety regulations or being greedy with space are especially unattractive behaviors. Air travel also calls for patience in loading and unloading.

The Motel and Hotel Guest

The most frequent complaint about hotel guests is loudness—either loud partying, loud music, or loudness in the halls and lobby. This usually only happens with immature people or people who have had too much to drink. If you experience hotel neighbors with these habits, you may appropriately ask the hotel manager to correct the situation. When you are compelled to report rudeness or unpleasantness, do so with tact and politeness.

As a welcome hotel guest you will want to be sure that any children in your party are well attended. And, of course, as an honest person, you never take hotel property and you avoid leaving the room in total chaos.

Using Public Facilities

Well-mannered people take responsibility for the care of public facilities—facilities that belong to everyone. They do not litter or mark on walls. They dispose of trash in proper receptacles. They are not loud (calling attention to themselves) and they do not dominate the public spaces. They do not cut in lines nor demand more for themselves than others are due. They are gracious and considerate of strangers just as they are to friends and family.

Traveling by Group

School groups and tour groups are excellent opportunites for traveling and for experiencing new and interesting sights. In order for these experiences to be satisfactory for everyone, there are guidelines for traveling in groups. Here are selected guidelines:

- Be generally considerate of everyone in the group.
- Remain quiet when the tour guide speaks.
- Be prompt for bus departures.
- Be cheerful in rotating seating on a tour bus that has a rotation system.
- Smoke only on breaks.
- Avoid being pushy and loud.
- Avoid taking excessive luggage.

- Take only the luggage you can manage unless the tour includes luggage service.
- Never congregate in the front area of the bus.
- Don't talk to the driver when the bus is moving.
- Avoid being a critic of areas and people being visited.
- Take every opportunity to learn about differences you encounter in new countries, among new people, and with new foods.

REMEMBER:

1. Travel is a great opportunity to learn about life and to enjoy living.
2. Travel is more satisfying when you have an attitude that appreciates differences.
3. As a polite traveler with good manners, you will be treated with more respect than those who are either ignorant of travel etiquette or inconsiderate of others.
4. *Travel when you have the opportunity and enjoy the experience!*

CHAPTER 5

At the Table

In this chapter:

1. a standard table setting
2. good manners when eating at a restaurant
3. ways to handle difficult foods

People who have good table manners practice them regularly, thus creating habits that make them feel comfortable wherever they may be eating. As a dinner guest in a private home or at a fine restaurant, there is no need for concern about correct behavior if you normally practice good manners.

The first thing to remember when considering etiquette for dining is that people eat for two reasons—first because they need food, but second, as a social event. Eating and talking together, whether in a home or in a restaurant, is pleasant to almost everyone.

Good posture is an important rule of good table manners. Without correct posture, no amount of knowledge about which fork to use or how to eat special foods is enough to make you attractive as you eat. Sit straight, with hands on the table, or in the lap, as needed for natural eating.

With good posture and an attitude of enjoying the company of others, as well as enjoying the food, you are ready to practice standard methods of eating. Here is a drawing of the way items are arranged in a standard place setting.

To the right of the plate are the knife (cutting edge turned toward plate), spoons, and cup and saucer. Above the knife are all glasses with the water glass above the knife.

To the left of the plate are forks and the napkin. Any silverware placed above the plate is for dessert. To remember this, practice setting the table at your home by these standards. Then it becomes second nature and you will never have to worry when you invite someone to a special meal that you have the table set correctly.

EATING IN RESTAURANTS

Standard manners at the table contribute to the enjoyment of a meal—both for the individual and for everyone at the table. When a person with really bad table manners eats with others, the bad manners not only make the person unattractive but also make other guests uncomfortable. Visualize a person who talks with his mouth open and full. The person across the table from this ill-mannered person sees the food as the person talks. This is a really gross sight! Or visualize the person who sits at the table, slumps in her chair, puts both elbows on the table, and scoops her food into her mouth without looking up to talk with others during the meal. Such a sight labels a person as one who has never given any thought to positive self-images.

Note the difference in these two postures:

Many people eat quite casually at home, but they are interested in presenting themselves attractively when they eat at someone else's home or when they eat in a restaurant. Here are some guidelines for eating attractively.

When eating at a restaurant remember these items:

- Wait at the entrance to be seated by a waiter. In a social situation women follow the headwaiter to the table, and men follow. The group hostess takes the seat pulled out by the headwaiter.
- It is permissible to ask for a different table if you prefer another, but do not insist on a change if none is easily available.
- In a large group, each individual gives his or her own order to the waiter. When the meal is a business one between a man and a woman, it is the responsibility of a woman to say to the waiter, "May we have separate checks, please."
- When giving your order to the waiter, be specific and avoid changing your mind. Try to be ready with your decision when the waiter comes to your table.
- Feel free to ask the waiter about any item on the menu that you do not understand. For example, say politely, "Can you tell me how the 'potatoes au gratin' are prepared?"
- Olives, cherries, or onions served in cocktails may be eaten.
- When an uncut loaf of bread is placed on the table, the host slices or breaks off two or three individual portions and then passes the bread basket around the table.
- The iced teaspoon is placed on a plate after it is used, as is all silver.
- Paper wrappers should be crumpled tightly and either tucked under the rim of a plate or placed on the edge of the saucer or butter plate.
- The usual way to call a waiter is to catch his eye and raise your hand, as if to say, "Attention." If he refuses to look in your direction, you may call, "Waiter," quietly, without attracting the attention of other diners. If he is too far away to hear you, say to another waiter who is passing by your table, "Please call our waiter."
- At the end of a meal a woman may apply lipstick, but other grooming should be done in the restroom.

- When a group enters a restaurant and sees people whom some know and others do not, they continue directly to the table, nodding or saying "Hello" as they pass. It is rude to stop and visit in the pathway of others.
- Complaints about food spoiled or incorrectly prepared should be made quietly, without attracting the attention of the other diners.
- To determine what is a finger food and what is not, use this rule: if it gets your fingers messy, use a fork or spoon; if it isn't messy, you may use your fingers. Common finger foods are crispy fried chicken, pickles, cake squares with no icing, cookies, and similar foods.
- Never use a toothpick in public, and *never, never* exit a restaurant with one in your mouth.
- Be generally considerate of others; avoid loud behavior that calls attention to yourself.
- In a very formal restaurant finger bowls may be brought to the table between courses. To use them correctly, dip the tips of your finger in the water and dry them on your napkin.

QUESTIONS AND ANSWERS

Here are questions frequently asked about good manners when eating in restaurants or in the homes of others.

Question: Is it all right to have seconds when I am a guest at a meal?

Answer: Yes. It is a compliment to the hostess to take seconds. At a buffet meal, be sure every guest has been through the buffet line before you go for seconds.

Question: What do I do with the foil that is around a baked potato?

Answer: Push it down around the potato (almost like forming a base for the potato).

Question: May I eat the peel on a baked potato?

Answer: Yes, if you are confident that the potato was well scrubbed before it was cooked.

Question: What can I do if I don't drink alcoholic beverages and everyone at the table orders wine?

Answer: Be confident with your choice, remembering that mature people and good friends respect the right of others to make their own choices. Do not offer an explanation for your choice just as you make no excuse when you decide not to drink coffee or tea.

Question: Do I wait until everyone at my table has been served before I begin eating?

Answer: Yes, unless the table is a long banquet table with dozens of people seated at it. In that case, wait until people on each side of you, and those across from you, have been serviced. Then you may begin.

Question: How do I know who will pay for the meals in a group party?

Answer: The person who organizes the group to eat out should make clear what kind of event it is—a "dutch treat," or an invitation to you to be their guest.

Question: When I am a guest of someone else at a restaurant, how do I decide what price meal I should order?

Answer: Because it is embarrassing to order an expensive steak and then hear the host order a baked potato or salad only, you may ask a question or two to get some clues for your choice. You might ask: "What do you recommend?" or "What looks good to you?" or you could say to the waiter when she comes for your order, "I'm not quite ready to order; you go ahead, Tom (host)." Notice the price range of what the host recommends or orders for himself. If these things do not give you a clue, choose something that is not the highest- nor the lowest-priced item on the menu.

Question: If I order wine for the table and the waiter brings the bottle to the table and asks me to give it my approval, what do I do?

Answer: The waiter will pour a small amount into your wine glass. Then you pick it up, look at it, pass it under your nose to test its aroma, and then you take a sip. After these actions, say to the waiter, "It's fine; we will have a bottle." The waiter then pours the wine for everyone at the table. Remember that the wine-tasting is an ancient ritual that developed when wine processing was not as sophisticated as it is today. In ages past, sometimes a bottle of wine would turn to vinegar, and to prevent having spoiled wine served to guests, the ritual was developed.

Question: Is it ok to eat with both knife and fork like the people from England eat?

Answer: Most people in the United States use the American style of eating; however, if you are accustomed to eating the English style, and that is the comfortable way for you to eat, feel free to do so. (With the English style the person holds the knife in the right hand and the fork in the left hand throughout the eating process. He pushes the food onto the fork with the knife and usually carries the food to the mouth with the fork upside down.)

REMEMBER:

1. Good table manners contribute to your image as a professional person.
2. Good table manners may be especially important if you are invited to eat at a restaurant as a part of a job interview.
3. People who practice good manners all the time will be more comfortable.

CHAPTER 6

As a Visitor

In this chapter:

1. ways to make yourself a person admired as a guest
2. considerations for informal and formal occasions
3. a welcome house guest (e.g., an overnight guest)
4. the benefits of being a "welcome guest"

To be invited into someone's home is one of the greatest honors that a person can receive. Visiting in the homes of others can be a pleasant experience if you are confident that you know how to conduct yourself. Here are some guidelines that hold true whether you are visiting in the homes of friends or family or you are visiting with new acquaintances. The guidelines relate to overnight visits as well as short day visits.

Approach a visit to another home with a positive attitude, expecting to be with interesting people who will welcome you. Of course, not every family, nor every home, is the same. But when you go into the homes of others you have the opportunity to observe various lifestyles, home styles, family behaviors, etc. Therefore, if you are to enjoy the experience, anticipate an opportunity to broaden your understanding of others and learn from the differences you encounter.

Use the following guidelines to show respect and appreciation when you visit others.

GUIDELINES FOR BEING A WELCOME GUEST

- Be prompt; arrive neither too late nor too early.
- Never bring uninvited guests.
- If you are detained, call ahead and explain.
- If you must leave early, give a quiet explanation to the hostess.
- Take care of hosts properly—avoid putting wet glasses on table tops, avoid leaning back in chairs, avoid putting feet on furniture, etc.
- Offer to assist, but do not insist.
- Call and give your regrets if you develop a really bad cold or other serious illness.
- When offered a choice, make one.
- Take responsibility for participating in the activity of the evening.
- Participate in conversation with as many guests as possible.
- Avoid long good-byes.
- Leave on time.
- If you know you cannot reciprocate, take a hostess gift.
- Thank the host and hostess.

A special note for contemporary visitors relates to beverages. It is not uncommon in our informal society to have a young guest arrive at someone else's home with a cup or glass of beverage from a local fast food place. That immediately sends a message to the hostess, something like this: *I guess he thinks I will not serve anything that he likes.* To be a welcome guest, leave commercial cups of beverage that you may have in the car.

THE ATTRACTIVE HOUSE GUEST

A "house guest" is a person who stays overnight in another person's home. There are four excellent rules for being a welcome house guest. They are:

1. Participate in the events planned for your visit. Show your interest in and be appreciative for the activities your hosts have planned for you. Be sure to take clothes versatile enough for a variety of activities.

2. In general, keep the schedule of the family you are visiting (e.g., go to your room when they go to bed, be ready to eat when meals are served, etc.).
3. Take care of the hosts' property. For example, rinse out the tub after your bath, pick up the papers after reading them, and return your empty drink glasses to the kitchen.
4. Send a thank-you note after the visit. Be sure to mention some specific things you enjoyed.

REMEMBER:

1. You are greatly honored by people who invite you into their home.
2. Always go for a visit with a positive attitude, expecting to find differences from the home in which you were reared. Appreciate the differences!
3. Good manners make you a welcome guest.

PART II

EFFECTIVE COMMUNICATION

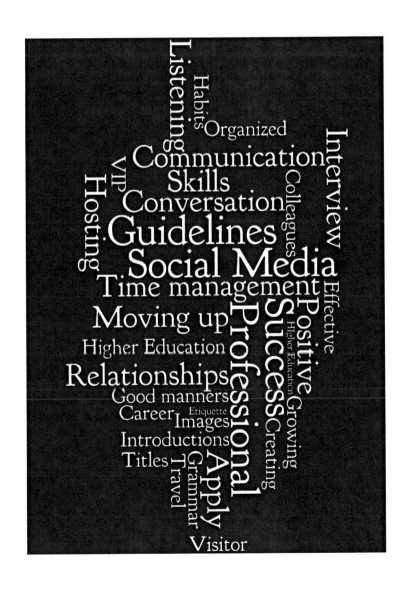

CHAPTER 7

Introductions and Titles

In this chapter:

1. making introductions correctly
2. showing deference to the elderly and the distinguished
3. using titles correctly

INTRODUCTIONS

Many people are insecure about making introductions. While there are guidelines for making introductions correctly, it is important to introduce strangers who are with you, regardless of whether you know the guidelines or not. Here are some simple guidelines for making positive introductions.

A Standard Introduction

Here is the correct way to make a simple introduction: "Michael Spurrier, I'd like you to meet Scott Gilbreath."

Notice that in that example, full names are used and there is no repetition of the names. A careful introducer says the names in a clear voice, using the full name of both people.

The people being introduced follow with one of a variety of comments, such as: "I am happy to meet you," or "How-do-you-do," or "Hello, Scott. I've heard good things about your work here."

They usually shake hands with each other as they respond to the introduction.

Polite people always *stand* when they are being introduced unless they are not able to stand comfortably because of age or illness. When a young person is introduced to a person who cannot stand, it is very gracious for him or her to sit beside the person and talk for a few minutes.

It is especially polite to follow the introduction with some information that will help the two people begin to talk together. The person who introduces Michael and Scott could follow with: "Scott, Michael is looking for someone to tell him about the New York Giants, and I told him you see most of the games. What are their prospects for this year's competition?"

Showing Deference with Introductions

The introducer can show deference to one person over another person in the way the introduction is made. However, when peers are introduced, it does not matter who is introduced to whom. In the example above, the introduction of two could just as correctly have been made in reverse: "Scott Gilbreath, I would like you to meet Michael Spurrier."

When you are introducing a young person to a much older person or when you are introducing a very important person, give deference to the elderly person and to the distinguished person. A person does that by calling the name of the older or distinguished person first, in this manner: "Great-Grandmother Johnson, I would like you to meet Beth Crocker." And in a similar manner: "Mr. President, I would like you to meet Joe Garrett."

Likewise, give deference to outsiders when introducing your family. "Mr. Sanchez, I would like you to meet my brother, Harold Castro."

When introducing people, use the name and title you expect them to use with each other. For example, if you are introducing a child to an older person, you would expect the child to use a title when speaking to the older person, so you would say, "Mrs. Culpepper, this is Bobby Jordan." Such an introduction indicates that you expect Bobby to speak to the woman being introduced as "Mrs. Culpepper."

If you forget a person's full name, introduce anyway, using the name you do remember: "Mrs. Jones, I would like you to meet Mrs. Burns."

Or perhaps you can only remember first names; if so, then you might say, "Harry, I want you to meet Winston." Or in the unlikely event you know the people but can remember neither name, you could improvise with something like, "I want you two to meet each other because I know you are both really interested in the Cowboys and you will enjoy sharing the experiences you have had with the team. Please introduce yourselves while I go get coffee for all of us."

MAKING OTHERS FEEL COMFORTABLE FOLLOWING INTRODUCTIONS

One important way you become more confident in making introductions and in meeting new people is to focus on them. By changing the focus from yourself to others, you become less nervous and more confident. You can begin to show interest in others by asking questions about their interests and their lives rather than by spending the majority of your talk time on your own interests. For example, someone you have met may ask, "How are you getting along with your new iPad?" By all means you will want to answer, but when you have shared a reasonable amount of information about your success and enjoyment of the new technology, then be sure to ask a question that will allow the other person to talk some as well. You might say, "What social media do you find most helpful in your work at the bank?"

Thoughtful people do not dominate the conversation. They do not engage in loud, raucous behavior, and they consider the needs of others. One way people do this is to be sensitive to them—sensitive to inclusiveness, to feelings, and even to physical needs. For example, if a person standing beside you appears to be sad, you might ask, "Has this been a bad day?" Or perhaps, "What are you looking forward to for tomorrow?"

APPROPRIATE USE OF TITLES

The question of how to use titles, or, in fact, whether to use them at all, usually comes up when you meet new people or when you are introducing people. If you are unsure about using a title, remember that it is safer to use a title than not to use one. That is true because you are much less likely to offend a person by giving him a title when he prefers first names, than you are by calling him by his first name when he expects his title to be used. Here are some guidelines for the use of titles:

- *Mr.* is always a correct title for a man. Of course if he has a unique title like *Captain*, you will want to use that title instead. Always use the highest title a person has unless he requests first names only. For example, it would be rude (and unwise for you) to call General Smith by the title Sergeant Smith.
- *Ms.* is a correct title to use for single women, for women whose marital status you do not know, and for women in professional roles.
- Titles for the clergy vary considerably from church to church; use *Mr.* if you do not know what is appropriate for a specific denomination.
- A physician is always addressed as *Dr.* However, a female physician may prefer to use her married name in social life. For example, in social settings, you might introduce a female physician in this way: "Mrs. Daniels, I would like you to meet Mrs. Franks. Mrs. Franks is Dr. Laura Franks, the oncologist in our local Medical Center."
- A person holding an academic doctorate may choose to use the title *Dr.* only in professional life; however, it is wise to use the *Dr.* title when unsure of the professor's wishes. If you are in a college class, address your professor as Dr. Smith unless you know for sure that she does not have a doctoral degree.
- Husbands and wives introduce their spouses by first name, never by title. For example, "This is my husband, John Smith," rather than, "This is my husband, Mr. Smith."
- When introducing someone's live-in partner, just use their names: "This is John Smith and Mary Jones." Leave out any reference to their relationship.
- Titles for stepparents depend on family preference. First names, nicknames, and, in some cases, Mother and Father, are all right to use. The words *stepmother* and *stepfather* are appropriate to use when introducing your parent's husband or wife. People who are

uncomfortable with those terms may choose to say, "This is my father's wife, Mary."
- Never give yourself a title when speaking to others unless the other person is a child or a student or a servant or a patient. When speaking to peers, say, "I am John Smith," not "I am Mr. Smith." On the other hand, a physician says to a patient, "Good morning, I'm Dr. Sanchez, your oncologist." Similarly, a college instructor says, "I'm Dr. Fenci, your language professor," and a school teacher says to students, "I'm Mrs. Sossbee, your math teacher."

COMMON TITLES

Table 7.1 shows some of the most commonly used titles.

Table 7.1. Commonly Used Titles

A university or college professor	Dr. Smith
A physician	Dr. Smith
A woman in business	Ms. Smith
A minister	Mr. Cason (or a title unique to the particular denomination, such as: 　　Father George 　　Brother Lewis 　　Pastor Brown 　　Bishop Harry 　　Reverend James
A teacher	Mr. Sanchez
A legislator	Mr. Woolridge, or in introduction, the Honorable Joseph Woolridge
The President of the United States	Mr. President

ADDRESSING ENVELOPES

Address envelopes with correct titles, as shown above. There are some unique cases; for example, occasionally a couple will have different last names. In such cases, the envelope should read: *Ms. Mary Smith and Mr. George Martinez*

When writing a woman's name, use her husband's name when you use *Mrs.* as the title (e.g., Mrs. John Smith).

On the other hand, if you wish to use her first name, use the title *Ms.* (e.g., Ms. Mary Smith).

In addressing a couple who both hold doctoral degrees, the envelope may be written this way: *The Doctors Hernandez;* or it could be written as *Dr. Robert Hernandez and Dr. Anna Hernandez.*

When a letter is addressed to a whole family, as, for example, in the case of a Christmas card, the address may read: *The DeMoss Family.*

REMEMBER:

1. It is always better to make introductions, even if you do not remember the rules, than it is to make no introduction when you are with people who do not know each other.
2. People appreciate being addressed by their appropriate titles.

CHAPTER 8

Practical Guidelines for Effective Communication

In this chapter:

1. conversation skills
2. listening skills

CONVERSATION SKILLS

Talking to others with ease and with good manners is an important skill for successful people. Talking comfortably seems to be natural for some people, but for others it is difficult. Even persons who feel they have no conversational weaknesses may find some of the information in this chapter helpful.

EFFECTIVE CONVERSATION

Effective conversation involves two activities: listening and talking. Both are essential. Being able to listen effectively is important because listening is a source of information, a way to show respect, and a way to gain power with others. It is a skill worth developing.

Listening

People perceive that you are listening to them by your body language and by your verbal responses. For example, visualize a secretary and a clerk talking together. Imagine that the secretary asks a question. As the clerk answers the question, the secretary checks his watch, glances away as someone enters the room, and adjusts his socks. How do you think the clerk feels about the amount of interest the secretary has in his answer? You know right away that the clerk quickly decides that the secretary is not interested in his answers!

On the other hand, if the questioner looks at a person who is answering and avoids distracting activities, the talker will believe that the questioner has a real interest in what he has to say.

In addition to body language, a good listener responds to the talker with a comment on the same topic. For example, if a person has been discussing software availability for a new computer, a careful conversationalist might say something like, "It's good to know about that package; I may look at it." On the other hand, the poor conversationalist may respond with another topic entirely unrelated to computer software. A comment like "Oh, the budget hearing has been called for this afternoon" leaves the talker to believe that the person who asked the question had no real interest in his answer.

You honor a person by listening to him or her and you show this in many ways. For example, sit beside him or stand near him as you listen. Certainly you will want to look at him while he speaks.

To make a child feel important, an adult may kneel near the child so that their faces are on the same level. Similarly, elderly people feel honored when younger people sit beside them for talking and for hearing what they have to say.

Good listening manners include these:

- Look at the person to whom you are listening.
- Make appropriate responses when the talker pauses.
- Avoid interrupting.
- Never correct the speaker's grammar.
- Avoid finishing stories and completing sentences for the speaker.
- Make a responsive comment about the topic when the speaker finishes.

Listeners usually *remember* what they hear if they can mentally associate the information with facts they already know. In the example above, the listener may remember the name of the software best if he determines he will remember it by associating it with something he already knows. Even better is making a written note about it while he is with the person who mentioned it to him. Another helpful technique is to repeat what you want to remember before you leave the conversation.

Talking

Participation is the key ingredient in effective conversation. Everyone speaks with ease and comfort to family and friends, but successful businesspeople must be able to talk with everyone—new acquaintances, teachers, clients, coworkers, and management—even the unfriendly, the uninterested, and occasionally the angry person. Inexperienced people may say that they would be happy to talk, but that they do not know what to say. Information is essential for good conversation. What are your sources of information?

Successful people note the headlines shown on their computer as soon as they first open it in the morning. They read, study, and listen to local and national news reports so that they will know what is happening in local schools, in the community, and in the workplace. Busy people recommend these as easy ways to learn what is happening in the world around them:

1. Become comfortable and skilled at using social media.
2. Read the front page of a daily newspaper each day.
3. Keep the car radio tuned to a station that gives news every hour.
4. Watch the news on television once each day.
5. Use the Internet to access information.

Some people keep a book with them wherever they go, so if they have wait time, as in a doctor's office or a laundromat, they can make use of the time to either enjoy a story or do some work.

Topics When Conversation Is Awkward

Sometimes young people say that they do not know what topics to mention to strangers or to people considerably older than they are. Here are topics of general interest with sample questions:

- Occupations: "Mr. Brown, what kind of training is required for a person working at your factory?"

- Local issues: "Mrs. Smith, why do you think so many people want curbside garbage pickup?"
- Local events: "Jim, how will your company fit into the Heritage Festival events?"
- Leisure: "Ms. Hernandez, do you play tennis?"
- National events: "Ms. Hernandez, what do you think about the number of presidential debates we are having this year?"

Levels of Talk

Remember as you consider topics to introduce into conversation that there are several levels of talk. Successful people strive to keep the majority of their conversation on the upper levels. Low-level talk is gossip, which is especially harmful to others. Gossip is unreliable and often it is harmful to the gossiper as well as to the person who is the subject of the gossip. In the business environment, gossiping can be professionally deadly. Too much gossiping causes a person to be characterized as a gossip. This is a negative label that everyone wants to avoid. The level of your talk reveals your interests, concerns, and knowledge.

Figure 8.1 Levels of Conversation

Special Business Considerations

A good conversationalist in family and social situations is usually a successful one at school and work. However, there are some additional guidelines for conversation in the workplace. For example, businesspeople should be cautious about what they say. It is better to say too little than too much. And when you need to express an opposite opinion, do so with tact. A person who has a different position from one she has just heard might respond with a comment like this: "That certainly is one approach we could take; however, I would like to suggest that we consider another one as well."

Posing a question in a tactful manner is a good way to introduce an opposing position. For example, if you are a part of a group planning a banquet and you feel the current plan is much too costly, you might say, "You people are making a terrible mistake with the plans—we will never raise the money for this and anyone who thinks we can is simply wrong!" Or you could, with much more likelihood of success, say, "I am feeling a real need to look at our cost and at how much money we have. Can someone help me understand our budget for this event?"

Reserve an open mind on issues. Discuss, but do not argue. It is a mark of superior minds to be able to disagree in a tactful and kind way. Make statements based on knowledge and experience, not just on conjecture.

Praise coworkers who do good work, and avoid being too critical. Do not tell a story at someone else's expense. A laugh is not worth a friendship or poor relations with coworkers. Likewise, it is a mistake to be overly sensitive. Guard against the temptation to think that others are talking about you.

Develop an image of a person who keeps confidences. Do not talk about one friend to another. Remember that a person who talks to you about someone else will talk with others about you.

Never criticize the place where you live, study, or work. As long as you are a part of an organization, be loyal to it. When you can no longer be loyal, consider a change.

IMPROVING YOUR COMMUNICATION SKILLS

If you have a goal of being able to talk with anyone at anytime, then you will want to develop standard speaking habits, accents, vocabulary, etc. This means speaking without grammatical errors and without strong accents. It also means having a vocabulary extensive enough to express yourself comfortably. A person with an inadequate, or limited, vocabulary often resorts to unattractive and unpleasant slang to express himself.

A person may begin to improve personal speaking skills by practicing sensitivity to language that is unique to the local area. Listen to the way people in your neighborhood talk, and you will soon identify local accents and phrases. Here are some examples of language that is substandard:

Table 8.1. Examples of Substandard Language

Substandard	Standard
I ain't got no cigarettes.	I have no cigarettes.
He don't love me anymore.	He doesn't love me anymore.
Me and my girlfriend went to the movie.	My girlfriend and I went to the movie.
Where is it at?	Where is it?
I loves chocolate candies.	I love chocolate candies.

EVALUATING YOUR OWN SPEAKING HABITS

Use these five questions to evaluate your speaking habits. When you do, you may find some changes you want to make.

1. Do you routinely make grammatical errors? The most common ones are:
   - Misuse of *I* and *me*:
     - Correct: John and I are leaving.
     - Incorrect: Me and John are leaving.
     - Correct: The call is for me.
     - Incorrect: The call is for I.
   - Ending a sentence with *at*:
     - Correct: Where is it?
     - Incorrect: Where is it at?
   - Incorrect verb form:
     - Correct: The girls are here.
     - Incorrect: The girls is here.
     - Correct: The boys, the girls, and one mother are here.
     - Incorrect: The boys, the girls, and one mother is here.
2. Do you tell dirty jokes?
   - Before you tell such a joke, ask yourself, "Will I offend someone who is listening?"
3. Do you use slang words that are offensive to some people?
   - If you use "bathroom" words or words related to sexual activity, you are probably offending someone. Think about changing your

slang words. No one wants to be characterized as a person with a "dirty mouth" but that can happen when a person is careless with words. It is easy to repeat dirty words after we hear others use them. Check your slang words. Words commonly used in some families may be offensive to people in other families.

4. Do you have a strong accent or regional speech?
    - An example of a regional accent is found in some regions where people may have speaking habits such as dropping the letter *g*. Thus *pudding* becomes *puddin*, and *fixing* becomes *fixin*, etc. Do you use regional slang that labels you? For example, many southerners speak of a group of people as *y'all*. This is a shortened version of *you all*. Now, southerners are proud to be from the south and take pride in their local characteristics; however, if, as individuals, people want to be clearly understood by all people, and if they do not want regional labels, they practice using standard phrases, words, and accents. If you want to correct an unattractive speech pattern, begin with only one or two items. Maybe you have discovered you use *I* and *me* incorrectly. To change your habit, plan how you will use the words and follow these steps to change your habit.
        ○ First, write several sentences using the words correctly, such as
            ▪ My friend and I went to the movie.
            ▪ Mom and I shopped for shoes.
            ▪ Keith and I like apples.
        ○ Next, when you are alone, say the sentences over and over until the phrases seem comfortable to you. If you hear yourself use the words incorrectly, force yourself to rotate the words in the sentence. If, without thinking, you say, "Me and Joe want to see a video," immediately rephrase the statement aloud, saying, "Oh, I mean, Joe and I want to watch a video."

5. Do you tell jokes about minorities?
    - This practice is not only unattractive but also disrespectful and harmful to others. An adult can lose his or her job if supervisors learn of this kind of talk in the workplace. The person who tells minority jokes also becomes characterized as a racist—a very damaging label.

D OFFICE TELEPHONES

Here are some guidelines for using home and office telephones.

1. Answer with "Hello" for the home telephone, but for the office, give your company's name followed by your full name.
2. Time your calls to avoid meal times. Likewise, call at a later hour on weekend mornings than on weekday mornings.
3. If you suspect you have dialed a wrong number, say, "Is this 214-1111?" not, "Who is this?"
4. Allow the telephone to ring about six times before you hang up.
5. If a person rings your telephone by mistake, be courteous, saying, "This is 564-1111. I believe you have misdialed."
6. If you get an obscene call, hang up immediately.
7. If someone calls you at an inappropriate time, be courteous but say, "I'm sorry to say I cannot talk right now; may I call you back in a few minutes?" (Be sure to return the call as soon as possible.)
8. When taking a message for another person, always write out the message carefully and leave it beside the telephone in the home or on the person's desk in the office. Take care to get the caller's name, number, and message. Note the time of the call, and add your initials.

PERSONAL LETTER WRITING

E-mail, iPhones, and cell phones have greatly reduced the practice of personal letter writing. However, letters are still appropriate for many purposes, and they are still valued. Handwritten letters are especially correct for thank-you notes and for letters of condolence. Below are samples of each of those. Notice that each of them contains at least three sentences.

The first sentence establishes the purpose of the note. For example: "Thank you for the billfold you sent me for my graduation." (It is important to *name* the item for which you are thanking the person.)

The second sentence says something positive about the item, such as: "The leather in it is soft and luscious and in a color just right for me."

The third sentence anticipates a continuing relationship: "I look forward to seeing you at our next family gathering."

Observe these three parts in each of the examples below.

January 1, 2004

Dear Mrs. Hernandez,

    Thank you so much for the fine briefcase. It is just what I will need in my new job as a salesperson. I look forward to having time to visit with you when I am in town again.

                                Sincerely,
                                Henry Hall

January 1, 2004

Betty,

    Congratulations on the wonderful success of the Fashion Show. It was marvelous, and you did a splendid job as moderator. Three sell-outs is not bad!!!

    Congratulations and thanks for all your many contributions to the community.

                                Sincerely,
                                Cathy Horne

January 1, 2004

Dear Sam,

    I was so sorry to hear about the death of your father. He must have been a fine man to have a son like you! Please accept my sympathy, and do feel free to call on me if I may be of help in any way.

                                Sincerely,
                                John Smith

GREETING CARDS

Many people send greeting cards for holidays and for friends who are ill. These bright, cheerful printed items are usually welcome. However, be sure you always write a personal note on each card. This removes the commercial stigma that comes from sending a card that carries only a message that was written by a stranger. Remember, too, that a handwritten sympathy card is the best form to use when you wish to send condolences to a person who has had a death in the family.

REMEMBER:

1. Positive communication skills, from conversational skills to writing skills, are keys to your being successful both socially and professionally.
2. Abide by institution or company policy in use of all types of communication, including social media, such as instant-messaging, Linked In, Facebook, Twitter, iPhones, and e-mail.
3. Evaluate your communication skills and, if needed, make a plan to improve your conversation and listening skills.
4. Despite the increasing use of social media for communication, do not lose your skills in the use of traditional forms of communication.
5. Handwritten thank-you notes and handwritten sympathy notes remain the mark of a considerate person.

CHAPTER 9

Communicating with Social Media

In this chapter:

1. guidelines for the use of social media
2. tips for e-mail etiquette and texting
3. wise use of video-chatting, Facebook, Twitter, and instant-messaging

Today almost everyone in your world, whether friends or business associates, is using several forms of social media. Whether you are using e-mail, Twitter, or video-chatting, or you have your own blog or are active on Facebook, there are tips for good manners (or etiquette) that make you more successful both socially and professionally.

TIPS FOR E-MAIL ETIQUETTE

- If you have given others your e-mail address, read your e-mail each day and respond as quickly as possible. A general guideline is the following: Reply to business e-mail within one day (just as you return telephone calls within a day). For personal (home) e-mail, return messages in at least one week.
- Begin a message with the name of the person you are e-mailing, such as: "Mary, thank you for the news about Sara's illness."
- Always close with your name. If you are e-mailing acquaintances rather than family or friends or coworkers, be careful to use your last name as well as your first name.

- Never put information in an e-mail that you do not want to be seen by others. Computer security still remains unreliable.
- Practice the same reservations in writing e-mail messages that you use in writing letters in regard to strong emotions. Remember, you can seldom recall a message after you hit the *send* button! If you are angry or if your message is on a sensitive topic, consider waiting to write, or consider a private conversation instead of a written message.
- Avoid using only uppercase in your message, because messages in uppercase are considered to be "e-mail shouting."
- Use business addresses for business purposes. Do your family and personal e-mailing on your home computer.
- It is all right to send congratulations to a colleague or friend via e-mail, and also you may send some thank-you notes via e-mail. Be guided in your decision by how important the gift, or action, was to you. For example, an e-mail is okay for thanking a person for helping you repair a computer problem. On the other hand, when your grandfather helps you buy a new car, a letter is much more appropriate.

FOR TEXTING, CONSIDER THESE GUIDELINES

- Texting can be deadly (when used while driving) as well as rude when used without thought of others.
- Text when you are alone rather than when you are with a group of people who are talking to each other.
- If you must answer an incoming text when you are with others, move to an area away from the group so that you will not interfere with their conversation.
- Never text in class, church, or at a formal presentation.
- Don't let texting replace face-to-face conversation.
- Exercise tact with what you say and how you say it. Strive for improved communication without offending anyone.
- If you wish to develop a closer relationship with a parent or grandparent, teach the person to text and use the method for frequent

short communication. The older person will be flattered that you are interested in texting with them.
- In a business meeting, class, or other gathering, you will not be able to disguise the fact that you are reading and sending messages. Wait, if at all possible, giving your full attention to the group activity.
- Excessive use of a tablet (such as the iPad) in business meetings is sometimes inappropriate; on the other hand, it is often a valuable tool for a meeting. Evaluate the situation to determine whether to take it with you or not.

FACEBOOK, TWITTER, AND INSTANT-MESSAGING MANNERS TO CONSIDER

- Few people enjoy hearing every detail of your day on Facebook.
- Use the *message* button, rather than posting on someone's "wall," to respond to individuals if you want to send some words that you do not want everyone to read.
- When offered an opportunity to "add a friend" to Facebook, it is all right to refuse by simply hitting the *ignore* button. Be guided by whether this person is someone with whom you want to build a relationship.
- While Facebook is generally considered for personal use, it may be helpful in some business relationships. Use caution in mixing the two.

VIDEO CHATS

Video-chatting is usually done among friends, but in some cases it is used for business purposes; for example, an interviewer might like to talk with you first via video chat before scheduling an office interview.

If you are initiating a chat, remember that it is rude to make an unscheduled contact. Set up the chat with the specific person you wish to talk with and, in preparation for the chat, give consideration to your appearance and to the area around you. Give your full attention to the person with whom you are chatting.

Instant-messaging is used in many businesses; however, two points of good manners are critical to its successful use. First, be brief, and second, be considerate of your colleagues' time and availability at a moment's notice.

As with all these forms of communication, abide by your school or company policy in using these devices.

REMEMBER:

1. Positive communication skills, from conversation to writing skills, from e-mail to the use of tablets, are keys to your success, both socially and professionally.
2. Every professional person needs social media skills.
3. Privacy and security are concerns with social media.
4. Abide by all company policies for the use of social media.

PART III

RELATIONSHIPS

Good manners
Death
Coworkers
Friends
Relationships
Birth

Managing conflict
Positive

Family

Divorce
Considerate
Sensitive to others
Major events
Weddings
Etiquette

CHAPTER 10

Guidelines for Relating to Others in a Positive Manner

In this chapter:

1. relating to people of all ages
2. the most valued personal quality
3. good manners in public places
4. in the coffee lounge
5. relating to the opposite sex in work environments

Developing and practicing skills in relating to others is the most important skill you can have for your own happiness and for your personal reputation. Successful people say these are the habits they developed for themselves when they were seeking a professional life.

1. *Always tell the truth.* Honesty is the number-one quality people want in individuals. Honesty means saying what actually happened, not what you wish had happened. It means not taking what does not belong to you and it means keeping your word by doing what you say you will do.
2. *Be tactful* if you must tell a person something that might upset him or her. For example, if a friend at school asks, "How do you like my new jeans?" and you don't think they look attractive, you might truthfully reply, "I think they are the tackiest pants I have seen all year!" However, you could be just as truthful but much more tactful and much less likely to hurt your friend's feelings if you replied, "They look like the latest new trend, but I liked the ones you wore yesterday best!"

3. *Never carry tales.* The person who repeats negative things people have said about someone else is the worst kind of gossip. In fact, a "tale-carrier" is to be avoided. Mrs. Walter Johnson, a wise old woman, once said about these people, "A person who brings a tale to you will carry one away." With this saying, she meant that a person who tells you gossip about someone else will probably tell someone else gossip about you.
4. *Control your anger.* Everyone gets angry occasionally, but the mature person has learned to control anger. The first step toward control is this: force yourself not to respond with angry words. You may need to say something like "I can't talk about that right now." Then later when you have control, plan how to respond calmly. Second, it is a mistake to write a note or e-mail in anger. Long ago the poet Ella Wheeler-Wilcox wrote a famous piece explaining this well-known fact: "You can never recall the written word." An old folk saying puts it this way:

> "Speak in haste
> Repent at leisure"

As a part of controlling your anger, practice never using physical violence. Fights at social gatherings usually mean expulsion or arrest, and in work places they usually result in loss of employment. Sometimes it takes a really strong person to walk away from an argument, but that is almost always better than getting into a fight. Likewise, bullies are no longer tolerated in educational settings or in the workplace.
5. *Show compassion and respect for others.* Studies always show that the qualities people want in friends, coworkers, strangers, or anyone else are, first, *honesty,* and, second, *consideration for others.* This is true for people of any age. It is true for people at school or at work, within the community or in social settings.
6. *Be a kind person.* People show that they are kind by being sensitive to others' needs. Here are some phrases that reflect kindness in our peers:

- "Let me help you."
- "I know this is a difficult time for you."
- "Good morning."

- "Great performance."
- "Your grandmother was one of my favorite people."
- "Tell me about it."

7. *Be a person respectful of others.* For example, never tell jokes about the elderly or the handicapped. Give respect to people in service roles, to custodians, and all people who work in your organization, regardless of their status. For example, we show respect to the custodians in our workplace by calling them, for example, Mr. Jones, rather than Buddy. Avoid criticizing in-laws or people who are different from you and your family.

8. *Be a gracious and considerate person.* Being gracious means being sensitive to the needs and feelings of people you are with. It means being responsive to these needs and feelings.

   Gracious people always ask politely for what they want, and then they reply with a thank you. Gracious people make generous use of both "thank you" and "please." They do nice things for other people. Consider the following actions as illustrations of a gracious person:

- Enrique helped John set up his new iPad.
- Mr. Burns opened the door for Mrs. Burns as they left the restaurant.
- Mrs. Burgdorf carried a loaf of bread to the new next-door neighbors.
- Tammy offered to pick up some groceries from the store for the elderly woman who lives in the next apartment.
- Mr. Sanchez took time to go by and tell the banquet speaker how much he enjoyed his presentation.
- John and Margaret sent a sympathy card when a friend's partner died.
- Suzie offered to feed the neighbor's dog while they were on vacation.
- Igor stepped back to let Henry, who was carrying heavy boxes, go first down the stairs.
- Rachel turned down her mp3 player when her housemate was reading.

9. *Avoid becoming a gossip.* Gossips are people who get great satisfaction from telling bad things about others. Gossips are not careful about checking for the truth of something they hear. They just rush to share it! They do not seem concerned about how another person might be hurt by their gossiping. They often try to pry personal information from people so that they can have a story to tell to others. It is hurtful to tell stories about people's personal problems.

10. *Avoid cruelty.* Cruelty can be all sorts of things from kicking a dog to telling lies about your best friend. Cruel people act in ways that hurt others. They do not seem to have empathy for the feelings of other people. A group of young adults was asked by the author to cite some examples of cruel behavior they had witnessed. Here are some things they mentioned:

- A group of men in the community held an illegal cockfight. The men took bets on which rooster would kill the other one.
- A skilled rider was arrested for beating his horse.
- Two teenagers placed ropes across the sidewalk and, hiding in bushes, pulled them taut to turn over bicycles when younger children rode by.
- Two girls sat happily on a park bench eating chocolates from a box, ignoring the requests of their younger sisters to have some of the candy.
- A businessman refused to pay for the work of two men he had hired from the labor pool.
- A woman required her house cleaner to work all day without giving her time to stop for a noon meal.
- A couple deliberately discussed the sad appearance of an overweight teenager within his hearing range.
- A teacher told a joke about minority students.

WHEN CONFLICT ARISES

Even when you practice all the communication habits you know to be effective, conflict will occasionally arise. Here are some ways people effectively deal with conflict.

Probably the most effective way to relieve conflict among friends is to say, "Let's talk." When you are calm and when a little time has passed since the disagreement, you can usually talk through the conflicts. Speak calmly and allow the other person to express his feelings without interruption. It may be helpful to tactfully correct misunderstandings. For instance, as you listen to what the other person says, you respond with a question for clarity. You might ask, "Is it true that you thought I said your proposal was refused? What I intended to say was that any of our reports could be refused depending on the thinking of the management."

After talking, the two people may still not resolve their conflict. They may just calmly agree to disagree on an issue. A way to end such a talk might be to say, "We may have to agree that we just hold different opinions on this matter; but we can still be colleagues working toward the goals of our organization."

Conflicts among friends are especially troublesome. There is seldom an issue or conflict so important that it is worth losing a friend. A wise man, J. Parry, once put into verse the value of making friends and holding on to old friends. Using a simple rhyme, he encouraged youth to make new friends (the "silver" in one's life) and to guard against abandoning old friends (the "gold").

Friends are one of life's greatest treasures, and the person who has friends should protect their friendships. Another famous saying from the poet E. Hubbard about friends expresses the idea that we do not have to agree with our friends on all issues, and we do not have to like everything about a person to be his friend.

> A friend is one who knows all about you
> And loves you just the same.

RELATING TO PARENTS

Parental love is one of the strongest forces in the world. Yet, sometimes as a mature and independent person, you may have conflicts with your parents. Some general ways to avoid as much conflict as possible are to spend time with your parents; talk to them at every opportunity. Share with them what is happening in your life; most parents have a great need to know that you are happy and successful in your profession.

They are honored when you occasionally ask for their advice. Ask if they ever had similar problems and how they handled them. The more you talk with your parents the less likely you are to have conflict with them. As with all communication, listen to your parents with a sincere desire to understand them. This is important with relationships with parents no matter how old they are or how mature you are.

Regardless of how near or far you live from your parents, stay in regular contact with them. That is the most ethical and most caring thing you can do as an adult child.

When your parents are assured that things are right in your world, they will be less apt to question you and express worries about you.

RELATING TO ELDERLY PEOPLE

Elderly people, just like other people, do not want to be victims of discrimination. Neither do they wish someone to call attention to their advanced age. Act around elderly people in the same manner as you relate to all adults. Unless they have severe health problems, their interests in life and their needs are much like their middle-aged peers. Do not assume they have limitations unless they are obvious.

Of course, you will want to make way for people in wheelchairs, on walkers, or on crutches. If an older person appears to be unsteady in walking, others are careful not to bump into them or rush them. The rudest thing young people mistakenly do around the elderly is to act as if they are deaf, or that they can no longer think clearly or understand current issues.

Retired people have often had rich life experiences and they have often built a great reservoir of wisdom. Smart young people try to learn from people who have already experienced what they have yet to encounter.

MAKING FRIENDS

As you think about relationships you may decide that you are not thoughtful in all your responses to people. You may want to work to make more friends or to improve relationships. Some specific ways to do that are to remember always to be tactful in what you say. Try complimenting at least one person each day. Be sure to thank people when they help you. Be an encourager and a sharer. For example, when appropriate, ask someone to help you with a task. (This may not be appropriate at work but can be very successful in your community life. For example, you might say to a friend or to a person whom you wish to know better: "Sam, I have to help put up a bus stop shelter with a group of volunteers. Would you be willing to help me one evening soon?") Don't forget to send congratulatory, sympathy, and celebratory notes to people when they are appropriate. Some people use their calendars to include birthdays and other important events in the lives of their family and friends. Facebook, too, can provide such information for you. All these tools help you to become a more friendly person.

PROTECTING YOUR POSITIVE PROFESSIONAL IMAGE IN THE COFFEE LOUNGE

The "break room" or "coffee lounge" is a great place for relaxing and for getting to know your colleagues on an informal basis. However, it is a part of the workplace; therefore, it is wise to guard your positive image there as elsewhere. For example, guidelines for teachers suggest that individuals visit the lounge during their conference period for a quick break, for a refresher, and for interacting with colleagues. But they should not spend the entire conference period each day in the lounge, because that projects the image of a lazy, or at least a procrastinating, worker. Perhaps the most important thing to remember is never engage in gossip during your break time. It is especially harmful for teachers to speak negatively about their students, other teachers, or the administration.

When a coworker approaches you with gossip about another colleague or client, a good answer is, "I'm sorry to hear that; I know the situation is troublesome for them." Then introduce another topic into the conversation.

RELATING TO THE OPPOSITE SEX IN WORK ENVIRONMENTS

Successful professionals keep their personal and sexual life separate from their work life. For example, they avoid dating people at work. However, if they do become romantically involved with a colleague, they are careful to keep their relationship outside the work environment. That is, they don't have coffee breaks as a couple, nor do they obviously take the part of the other in a company discussion, nor do they show affection with each other in the office.

Successful professional people are always careful to avoid any form of sexual harassment. "Sexual harassment" is generally considered to be any action with sexual context that is unwanted by others. Such things involve language, touching, and suggesting special rewards for special favors. Even certain "looks" can, in some cases, be construed as sexual harassment. Jokes often fall into this category without any individual harassment intended by the unthinking joke teller.

A worker who feels harassed should report the problem to his or her superior or to the human resources administrator.

REMEMBER:

1. Your relationships with friends, family, and coworkers affect your feelings of well-being and your success in reaching your goals.

CHAPTER 11

Responding to People Who Are Experiencing Major Life Events

In this chapter:

1. how to respond to people who are experiencing happy events in their lives as well as sad events
2. appropriate gift-giving
3. language for difficult times

Being sensitive to friends and acquaintances when they are celebrating special events or when they are suffering from serious problems is the mark of a mature person. Celebrations that call for the attention of family, friends, and acquaintances include graduation, birthdays, marriages, the birth of babies, and special anniversaries. On the other hand, sad and troublesome events such as divorce, serious illness, and death also call for attention from family, friends, and coworkers. As you think of your responses to these events, consider these ideas.

GRADUATION

The graduate may want to send invitations or announcements of the graduation services to friends and family. Send them three or four weeks in advance, and send them only to family and close friends.

It is rude for the person who receives such an invitation to ignore it. You may wish to send a gift, but gifts are not mandatory. However, if you choose not to send a gift, do send a note of congratulations.

As a graduate, you will want to send thank-you notes for any gifts you receive as soon as possible after the gift arrives.

MARRIAGE

When you receive an invitation to a wedding, respond with a gift appropriate to your level of friendship and to your budget. If you cannot attend the wedding, respond with regrets. If you do attend, be sure to choose what you will wear in consideration of the type of wedding planned (e.g., formal, informal, outdoors, in a church, or in a home). It is rude to wear something that looks as if you are trying to draw attention away from the bride. That is the reason that few guests at a wedding dress in white. That color is reserved for the bride.

It is also good manners to avoid taking an uninvited guest to a wedding.

BIRTH OF A BABY

When someone in your family or among your friends has a new baby, respond with a card of congratulations, a gift, or a visit to the hospital. Never ignore this happy event in families of your friends. If the mother is a coworker, it is appropriate to send a group gift or card of congratulations, but it is often a way to share in the congratulations without excessive expense.

GIVING AND RECEIVING GIFTS

Be a gracious receiver of gifts as well as a generous and considerate giver of gifts. Give gifts to encourage, to thank, to congratulate, to bear good wishes, to cheer, or to celebrate. Almost everyone enjoys receiving gifts, and often it is not the cost of the gift that makes it important. Rather it is the thought behind the gift. A gift is most important when it represents the sincere feelings of the giver. For example, if you want to give your grandmother a CD of music, consider her taste in music rather than yours. Perhaps you know she likes country western, and while you like only rock and roll, choose for her what you think she will most enjoy.

When you receive a gift, be sure to show appreciation and to thank the giver. If you are given the gift in person, open it and thank the giver at the time. On the other hand, if the gift is mailed or delivered to you, be sure to write a thank-you note as soon as possible.

Conversely, a professional person never accepts a gift that can be construed as a bribe. For example, once a teacher was visited by a father of one of his students, and during their conversation the father said, "I will be happy to fill your freezer with steaks if you will help my son pass his math course." The teacher, behaving in the way all professionals would to such an offer, replied, "No, thank you. I could not accept, but I will welcome your son in the tutoring sessions that are held each week for all math students." (Never give a gift in a way that it can be construed as a bribe.)

DIVORCE

When you learn that an acquaintance or coworker is getting a divorce, respond with good manners and consideration. Divorce brings unhappiness and various problems for the couple involved, for any children in the family, and for people close to the couple.

Good manners prevent people from prying or gossiping about the event. It is also important not to drop the couple from your social circles. When people are having family problems, they need friends more than ever. Respect their privacy but be available if your help and friendship are needed.

It is extremely important for the person experiencing family conflict to avoid bringing the problem into the workplace. In work full attention to work responsibilities is often excellent therapy for people who are grieving from a death, or are troubled with family conflicts.

SERIOUS ILLNESS

When a family suffers serious illness, considerate friends call to ask how they may be helpful. Sometimes visits to the home or to the hospital are in order. At other times, flowers to the hospital or food to the home are appropriate ways to show concern. Try to make your response according to the real needs and wishes of the family.

DEATH

When friends or neighbors or other acquaintances have a death in the family, respond to them in caring, considerate ways. The caring response of others is as important to a person who is grieving as an antibiotic is to a person trying to recover from a physical infection.

You will want to respond in a way that is appropriate to the closeness of your relationship. For example, if someone in your next-door neighbor's family dies, you will want to call on the family as soon as you learn of the death to ask how you may be helpful. Often, simple things, like mowing the front yard or making telephone calls or caring for a child, are greatly appreciated.

Various responses show respect: a visit to the home, a visit to the funeral home where you may sign the guest book, sending flowers, taking a gift of food to the home, or simply sending a note of sympathy. Today it is possible to register condolences via online facilities. Close friends and family will, of course, attend the funeral services. Today, many people send a memorial to a favorite charity instead of sending flowers. Either is correct, and if you know the wishes of the family, of course you will want to honor them.

If you choose to attend a funeral, dress in clothing that shows respect for the solemn occasion. Women avoid bright, bold-colored garments, and men wear a coat and tie.

After a death, it is important to remember that the grieving person still needs attention. Perhaps a visit, a call, or an invitation to dinner will be appreciated.

What to Say

Sometimes people do not respond to a grieving person or family because they have insecurities about what to say. Remember, if you are puzzled about how to talk to a person who has just had a death in the family, what you say is not important. What is important is your presence. Sometimes, no words—just a hug—is all that is needed. Or something like, "I've been thinking of you since I learned about Bob's death."

When a young person in a family has died, adults are often comforted from hearing from other young people that their child was special to his or her friends. Something like "Mrs. Chavez, Enrique was liked by everyone in our class; we will all miss him so much" means a great deal to grieving parents.

REMEMBER:

1. A mature person responds appropriately to friends and coworkers who are experiencing one of life's major events.

PART IV

PROFESSIONALISM

Independent
Coworkers
Lonely
Responsibility
Friends
Freedom
Time management
Social life
New skills
Academics
Job success
change
Success
Self-management

CHAPTER 12

Interview Skills

In this chapter:

1. best practices for gaining admission to institutions for higher education
2. preparing for a job interview
3. interviewing successfully
4. follow-up

APPLYING FOR ADMISSION TO INSTITUTIONS OF HIGHER LEARNING

Begin your search for continuing university studies by going online to learn about options for study in your chosen profession. Most universities have virtual tours online. By using this tool, you can explore many more universities than you can physically visit, and you can make a better choice of those you do want to visit after making the virtual tours. Today, you can do much online that once required time on campus.

In addition to considering your field of study, give consideration to finances. For example, if you go out of your state to college, the tuition, as a rule, will be more than it is within your state. Think about private universities versus state-supported universities—usually private universities are smaller and more expensive than the state-supported ones. "Net price calculators" are included among the online tools to help you understand costs of the study you are considering. These may be helpful to you if finances are a consideration. Grants and scholarships are often available for both beginning students and returning students. Counselors at the university will have information about them.

Preparing for Campus Visits

1. Make your appointment; be on time; dress neatly but comfortably (you will do lots of walking); carry writing material and a tote bag for the materials you will receive.
2. If the institution you choose requires an interview, follow the recommendations for successful interviews as given below, being sure to take transcripts and other required materials. Most private universities require interviews; on the other hand, many state universities require only that the student present evidence of the state requirements for entering the university.

GOOD MANNERS WHEN SEEKING WORK OR WHEN SEEKING ADMISSION TO COLLEGE

Good manners are always important, but they are never more important than when you are seeking a job or seeking admission to a specific institution of study. Regardless of other skills, often a person is not offered a position because he/she does not present a positive self-image. Consider interviews as opportunities to exhibit your skills in relationships and your knowledge and skills related to the position you are seeking.

PREPARING YOUR RESUME

You will no doubt look at sample resumes as you prepare your own. Perhaps you may also seek the advice of a person experienced in resume writing. Regardless of how you prepare your document, you will want to follow these principles for excellence in resume writing:

- Make the visual appearance of the resume neat and orderly.
- Organize data carefully.

- Be sure that everything on your resume is accurate. People who are not truthful in representing themselves can do irreparable harm to themselves for years to come.
- Always ask permission of persons you wish to use as references. It is considered extremely poor manners for a person not to ask permission and thus have a person learn they are one of your references only when a potential employer calls them to inquire about your abilities.

FINDING A PROSPECTIVE EMPLOYER

Several sources of information about job possibilities are available—college and university placement offices, newspaper want ads, commercial placement services, word-of-mouth from friends or family, and direct contact with personal officers. Look at all these as possibilities when you seek employment. Then approach the potential employer appropriately.

A successful interview occurs in three steps. These steps are outlined below.

Before an Interview

1. Prepare an attractive, accurate resume.
2. Learn as much as you can about the company or institution where you are applying.
3. Get clear directions for getting to the site of the interview and, if possible, learn the name of the person with whom you will interview.
4. Practice answering commonly asked interview questions.
5. Plan what you will wear to be appropriately and professionally dressed.
6. Decide what your best qualities are and how you will sell yourself.
7. If your interview is for admission to an institution of higher education, be prepared to talk about your skills, work experience, and extracurricular activities, as well as previous courses and grades.

8. Plan questions to ask about the company or institution that you are interviewing.
9. Leave the questions about finances for the time after you have talked about other concerns.

Dressing for a Successful Interview

- Groom yourself carefully; give special attention to haircuts, hair styles, and facial hair.
- Choose clothing that represents the profession you wish to enter.
- Avoid:
  - Garments that suggest a "sexy" look
  - Excessive body-piercing and tattoos

Conduct Yourself with Good Manners and Good Judgment during the Interview

- Never smoke or chew gum in an interview.
- Walk and sit with good posture.
- Shake hands with a firm grip.
- Look at the interviewer with eye-to-eye contact.
- Answer questions honestly.
- Be positive and enthusiastic.
- Avoid misrepresenting your abilities and skills.
- Speak clearly and distinctly.
- Never criticize former teachers or employers.
- Be prepared to describe some positive features of the institution where you received your education.
- Be prepared to tell why you want this job and what you can do for the organization if you are employed.
- Be prepared with some questions you wish to ask the interviewer.

After the Interview

After the interview, write a thank-you note to the interviewer. Here is a sample of one.

Dear Ms. Smith:

   Thank you for yesterday's interview for a position as a sales representative for your organization. Your description of the company was particularly interesting to me. I look forward to hearing from you about my opportunity to work for Smith, Jones, and Brown.

>Sincerely,
>Harry Hardeman

REMEMBER:

1. People who prepare careful, honest, and neat resumes have the best chance of getting the position they seek.
2. There is a positive relationship between the number of resumes or applications you send and the job offers you receive. Send many and thus give yourself more opportunities for choice.
3. Practice interview skills before going for an actual one.
4. First impressions are hard to change; always be prepared for a good first impression.

W WORKS WITH ENTHUSIASM

O ORGANIZED

R RESPONSIVE TO CLIENTS

K KNOWLEDGEABLE

CHAPTER 13

The Professional at Work

In this chapter:

1. principles of professional behavior
2. what the public expects of professional workers
3. what employers want from employees
4. what coworkers want from colleagues
5. resigning

Career specialists confirm that more people lose their jobs because they lack interpersonal skills than because they lack work-related skills. Mindful of that, professional people should give careful attention to their behavior at work and in their communities. The principles that guide relationships and behaviors at work apply regardless of assignment. For example, whether you are a teacher, an administrator, or a worker in some other profession, the principles are valid.

PRINCIPLES THAT GUIDE SUCCESSFUL PROFESSIONALS

Every profession has a code of ethics. For example, teachers and other educators are taught their code in classes that prepare them for certification, and copies are readily available from their state association. Other professions have similar ethical codes that guide their practice. Regardless of the profession, in general, codes of ethics for professionals have these principles embedded in their guidelines.

- honesty
- personal responsibility
- consideration of others
- loyalty to the profession, to their employer, to their colleagues, and to their clients
- development of the appropriate level of skills for the individual assignment
- personal growth and improvement
- contributions to the profession

The public holds people who are employed in professional roles, whether in medicine, law, education, or in service, to the high standards shown in these principles. The successful professional takes pride in abiding by the code of ethics of his profession.

EXPECTATIONS OF MANAGEMENT

Having positive relationships with people who are your supervisors or other professional leaders is critical to your success. As soon as possible, learn what the expectations for you are from the person to whom you report. Teachers, like other professionals, need to know where their immediate superiors place highest value. Perhaps for a school principal it is test scores, or discipline, or teamwork. When you know these values and priorities, you are equipped to be productive in the organization.

Remember, too, that in most professional roles it is unwise to do those things that highlight your work above that of the person to whom you report. Focus on working as a team, and then give the team, or your leader, credit for the successes.

EXPECTATIONS: WHAT COLLEAGUES LIKE

Surveys among workers show what work-related behaviors people like and what they dislike among their colleagues. Honesty, or personal integrity, is the number-one personal quality desired in all roles. That is especially true at work. For example, an ethical teacher would not change grades for a friend's child without academic cause. With the same ethical code of honesty, a professional builder would not take company equipment for personal use.

Honesty is also valued in what we say as well as in what we do. Recent criminal charges against workers in high places have proven the need for honesty in the workplace. Here are some ways to develop a reputation for honesty:

- Keep your promises. If you find you cannot carry out a task you promised, contact the person to whom you made the promise as soon as possible and explain the circumstances that have caused you to change your commitment.
- Tell the truth. Don't tell an untruth to impress your supervisors or to protect your colleagues. Lies are always found out.

Another expectation relates to the workplace itself. People, in general, like to work with others who keep their materials, equipment, and workspace neat and organized. A messy workspace is distracting and irritating, and in some cases, such as in medical fields, it can be deadly. Clutter often means the difference in a productive worker and a frustrated, low-producing worker. Coworkers want work partners who keep an orderly workspace—one that does not interfere with others' work and one that contributes to the overall impression of professionalism for the unit.

Workers like colleagues who show responsibility by coming to work on time and by being busy while they are at work. Professional people work "by the job, not by the clock." For example, it is irritating to have colleagues who spend a lot of time surfing the Internet without purpose instead of doing their work, or who spend excessive time talking on the telephone about personal matters, or who take excessive breaks, or who go home early at every opportunity. Other workers feel that they are cheated by having to cover for these workers who "steal" company time. In other words, it is the responsible worker who is respected.

All coworkers want pleasant colleagues who are positive, able to control their emotions, and who use appropriate language for the workplace. Similarly, people want not only pleasant, positive associates but also safety and security in the work environment regardless of whether that safety comes from the physical environment or from the behavior of coworkers. Countless cases of sexual abuse confirm this critical need of all workers in whatever their profession.

WHAT COWORKERS DISLIKE IN OTHERS

In the workplace, there are unattractive behaviors that responsible people avoid. They include behaviors such as bragging about themselves, their families, or their possessions; insensitivity to the feelings and situations of others; and gossiping. Of course, sexist behavior, whether it is verbal or physical, is one of the most serious behaviors in the work world. And, finally, workers in all areas report their disgust with colleagues who take credit for the work of others.

WHAT EMPLOYERS WANT FROM EMPLOYEES

- loyalty to the company
- ability to work with others
- motivated, energetic workers
- knowledgeable workers
- problem solvers
- productivity
- honesty
- appropriate communication in the workplace

RESIGNING FROM A POSITION

You may resign a position for many reasons, such as a better job, a family move, illness, or by request of your organization. Whatever the reason, resign with dignity and in a positive manner. Give consideration to the appropriate time for your departure. For example, if teachers plan to resign, they need to make their leaving date effective at the end of a semester if that is possible.

Send your letter of resignation in a timely manner, stating the effective date. Before you send the letter, learn company policy on times for resigning. Because schools are not year-round, some may wish teachers who plan to leave to announce that early in the semester before they are to leave. On the other hand, many companies ask only for a two-week notice.

In your letter of resignation, give some positive reason for your leaving. Write something complimentary about the company as well as about your colleagues. You may want to express special appreciation for events that have occurred during your time with the organization or perhaps for some skills and knowledge you have acquired while you were with the organization.

Continue your professional practice of not making derogatory remarks about the organization where you have worked.

REMEMBER:

1. Ethical principles guide the successful professional.
2. Relationships matter in all workplaces.
3. Knowing expectations leads to professional success.

CHAPTER 14

Selected Professional Responsibilities

In this chapter:

1. professional presentations
2. leading meetings
3. group decision making
4. social responsibilities at work

MAKING A PRESENTATION TO A GROUP

Guidelines for Presenters

Most professional people are called on, from time to time, to make presentations to groups. To do that successfully, consider the following guidelines.

Plan your presentation carefully; make notes that you can glance at and read as you talk to the audience.

Plan visual aids appropriate for the facility and the audience.

Time your presentation so that it fits the allotted time.

Go early and check the room for podium, screens, microphones, and other technical arrangements. Be sure the room is in order, knowing that a light, attractive, and comfortable room sets the stage for success. (As well, by going early, you may have an opportunity to meet some early arrivers. If the space is small enough for you to meet them, shake hands with several people and say a word of welcome or a word of thanks for your being invited to speak to them. This sets the tone for acceptance by the audience.)

When you are introduced, approach the podium with a posture that communicates excitement at sharing important information with colleagues. Pause at the podium; look out at the audience; make eye contact with various individuals; smile, and then begin your introductory remarks.

You may want to begin by making some complimentary remarks about the group to whom you are speaking. Then focus the presentation by telling the audience what the main topic is and what major points you will make. Tell the audience how the information may be helpful to them.

Present the well-organized ideas and facts in an orderly manner with as little reading as possible. Only reports that involve security or vital statistics need to be read. If you use a PowerPoint presentation, do not read it verbatim (if you do, your audience will read ahead of you and the whole speech will quickly become boring). Use PowerPoint to keep the audience focused and, where needed, to show critical facts or numbers.

Do use some form of visual aids, placed in view of everyone. Those that cannot be seen across the room are extremely frustrating to an audience. Refer to your visuals, but, again, use them only to focus the audience on the points you are making as you talk.

Speak in a conversational tone showing pleasure at the opportunity to share your information. Take comfort in the fact that you probably know more about your topic than anyone in the audience and remember that the audience has chosen to come to hear what you have to say. These attitudes build your confidence and improve your presentation.

Distribute handouts *after* the presentation; otherwise individuals will read while you talk.

Summarize with the same enthusiastic, positive approach you used to introduce the presentation.

LEADING MEETINGS

When you are chairman of a committee or president of an organization, or simply the leader of a team at work, organization is the key to your success. Knowledge of parliamentary procedure will also be critical for smooth operation of the meetings that may involve motions, voting, etc. *Robert's Rules of Order* (by Robert, Honemann, and Balch) is the standard resource for ways to conduct a meeting. Many professional people have that resource available when they are preparing for such a meeting.

Before the meeting it is important that notices be sent, in a timely manner, to every person expected to be at the meeting. Select a time appropriate for all participants and let them know the beginning hour and the projected ending time. Make a clear and concise agenda with copies for each member of the group. If individuals are expected to present new materials or proposals at the meeting, be sure they have an agenda ahead of time.

Go early to the meeting location and be sure that tables, chairs, visual aids, handouts, etc. are in place. Take extra agendas, even if you have already distributed them, in case someone does not bring theirs.

Begin on time. If you choose to wait for latecomers, thinking to be considerate of them, remember that you are probably being inconsiderate of the many who came on time. The leader who has a habit of beginning and ending meetings on time will be respected. Welcome the participants; make introductions if needed; restate the purpose of the meeting; and be sure there is a person to record actions of the group. If appropriate, set the ground rules and emphasize your desire for full participation.

After reports, discussions, decisions, etc., make a clear agreement on responsibilities that each participant will accept. Establish a timeline for completion. Thank members for their attendance and invite them to see you for further discussion if they wish to do so as they work on their accepted assignments. Set the time for the next meeting if another one is in order.

After the meeting, make a report to the superior who gave you the leadership assignment. Work with the meeting recorder to copy and send minutes to all participants. Follow through on the commitments you made just as you expect other members to keep their commitments.

GROUP DECISION MAKING

Knowing how to reach a group decision is critical to effectively leading a meeting. Decisions may be made by a group either by *consensus* or by *vote*. Consensus is used when, after general discussion, it appears that everyone in the group agrees with a specific course of action. When the leader perceives that is the case, she simply says, "Shall we agree by consensus on this action?" If everyone says "yes," then the minutes of the meeting record the decision. On the other hand, if someone says, "No, I will be more comfortable if we vote," then a motion is in order.

To manage a motion correctly, the chair recognizes a member of the group who has raised his hand. The person called on then states the action he wishes the group to take in the form of a motion, such as "I move that we assign the task of the holiday social to the communication subcommittee." Some member of the group must say, "I second the motion," in order for the process to continue. If no one seconds, the leaders say, "The motion is lost for want of a second," and the meeting moves on with another agenda item.

If there is a second, the leader calls for discussion. When it appears that all in the group who wish to speak to the motion have done so, the leader calls for a vote. The topic of the motion is either accepted or rejected by the vote.

It is inappropriate for the leader to make a motion. Also, when a motion is made and seconded, discussion and eventually a vote must follow.

REMEMBER:

1. When you have opportunities for presentations and for leading meetings, refresh yourself on guides for success.
2. Take advantage of the many resources that are available for such responsibilities.
3. If the meeting is to be formal, may involve conflicting ideas, and may involve a great deal of parliamentary procedure, refresh yourself ahead of time by reviewing *Robert's Rules of Order*. These are available in all libraries and you may get the information you need online (www.robertsrules.com).

CHAPTER 15

Social Responsibilities at Work

In this chapter:

1. greeting a visiting client
2. planning and hosting a company event
3. hosting a company VIP

WELCOMING A CLIENT TO YOUR OFFICE

Making clients, whether they are students or adults, feel welcome at your organization is critical to your success and to your company's success. That is accomplished first of all by employees having, and being able to communicate, an attitude of appreciation for the client.

When a client comes to your company or school to see you, the receptionist will no doubt alert you. It is very appropriate—in fact, it is recommended—that you go personally to the office to greet the visitor. Shake hands, welcome her, and lead her to your office. Offer a chair, say a few works of general welcome, and then proceed with the purpose of the visit.

You will want to do as much as possible to assure the client that you have an interest in her problem and you will do all you can to be helpful. The most important thing she needs, first of all, is to be heard. Listen attentively until you understand the concern. Often a client just needs to talk with you—to express her concerns. Many need to know several options. Even for those cases when you must give a negative answer, do so with tact and consideration for the person who is hearing unwelcome information.

HOSTING AN EVENT FOR YOUR ORGANIZATION

Many professional people are assigned the responsibility of planning and organizing a social event for the company. Perhaps it may be a retirement party, an anniversary celebration, an award ceremony, or another similar event. For example, a teacher may be asked to host a retirement party at the end of the school year.

When you are asked to host an event for your organization, get specific information from the person who gives you the assignment. You will want to know the date, the budget, the administration's expectation for the level of formality, who is to be invited, and a suggested location for the event. Some organizations allow for alcoholic beverages; others do not. You will want to ask about that as well. You will need to know, of course, if you are to work alone or with a committee. Ask if you will actually serve as host during the event or if someone from the organization, for example, the school superintendent, will be at the door to greet guests.

Working alone, or with a committee if there is one, make plans as soon as possible. Consider:

1. date and time
2. location
3. guest list and invitations (when to mail or distribute)
4. food and drink to serve
5. flowers
6. program
7. clean up

Make a chart of responsibilities with duties, date to be accomplished, and persons assigned to each duty. Post the chart in an appropriate place for all involved to see. Periodically (and tactfully) check with individuals on your committee to determine if they may need anything from you in order to accomplish their assignment.

Go early to the place of the event to check to see that everything is in order and to have time for last-minute needs or changes. Check to see that everyone is in place for the door, the table, the awards, etc.

After the event, thank all your workers and give a report to the person who gave you the assignment. Express appreciation for your opportunity to participate in the company event.

HOSTING A VISITING VIP

Principles and other managers often ask teachers or other workers to help host a person who is to visit your organization. For example, a teacher may be asked to pick up and transport the visiting accreditation team. If you are asked to host a VIP (very important person) for your organization, get special instructions from the person who gives you the assignment. In addition to the person's name, position, and purpose for the visit, you may be allowed to see a vita. All this will be helpful as you interact with the person. Ask about "pick up"—will the person come by air or car? If by air, will a car be available for your use or will you use your own (clean, of course)? Ask questions such as:

- What is the airport, gate, and time for the arrival?
- Where am I to take the person?
- Am I responsible for getting her a hotel room, and if so, where?
- Am I responsible for getting her to her meetings throughout her stay; if so may I have the visit agenda?
- Where am I to take the person?
- When do I return her to the airport?
- Are there other duties associated with her visit?
- What is the budget for the travel and hotel?

To be a host who is appreciated by both your organization and the visitor, be on time or early for each pick-up; check out the hotel room; and have a flowers (and perhaps a basket of fruit and crackers) in the room. It is also a good idea to have company materials as well as general reading material in the room. If the person is to go on her own to some meals, give her names of nearby restaurants. When you return her to the airport, be sure she has the appropriate materials from your organization as well as her own briefcase and luggage.

Finally, give your manager a report of the completion of the task. Your manager may appreciate a debriefing of what was said on the way to the airport if it is related to the organization and the purpose of the visit.

REMEMBER:

1. Clients, and the way they are treated, are critical to your success and to the success of your company.
2. Much serious and important business may be conducted at an organization's social events.
3. The first person a visitor sees in an organization has a strong influence on the visitor's impression of the firm.

CHAPTER 16

Growing Professionally

In this chapter:

1. self-management in professional life
2. time management
3. unique relationship concerns
4. moving up the career ladder

Success as a professional person, just as success as a university student, is dependent on self-management. Independent living, time management, relationships, further education, technology, housing—all present opportunities for success or failure.

SELF-MANAGEMENT IN INDEPENDENT LIVING

Management of finances, time, housing, food, time, professional clothing, social life, and family life requires planning and self-discipline.

When one begins a new job, resources may be limited; if so, there are three options to managing your resources.

1. Get more resources (a second job, a partner to share housing, a gift from parents, etc.).
2. Use more efficiently the resources you have (e.g., carpooling, preparing meals at home, etc.).
3. Lower your standards (e.g., buy a lower-cost car, take fewer vacation trips, etc.).

MONEY MANAGEMENT

Many new professionals see money as their most difficult resource to manage. That may be the case for you. If so, begin to address the problem by keeping a record for one month (or perhaps more) of your expenditures, and then make a financial plan or budget. Such a plan is a critical task for the new professional. Stay within budget guidelines overall, even though some items may increase as needs change. That increase can be balanced with a decrease in another area.

TIME MANAGEMENT

Time management is critical to your success and time-management principles set the stage for satisfying use of your time. It is only good management to honor your time, the time you give to your work, and the time you share with others. Here are the principles.

Good time managers are *sensitive to time*. If you are not, practice little things like learning how long it takes to get from your home to your place of work, or how long it usually takes to do daily assignments. See how often you can guess the time of day without looking at your watch. All these tricks help you become more time sensitive.

Good time managers *set goals* for each day. They prioritize them and decide how much time they will give each one.

They *delegate work* when it is appropriate. The ability to delegate is a critical skill for managers. For example, the college professor with a good secretary can be much more productive in the area of research and writing than one who has no help or poor help.

They *refuse to waste time*. Time wasters include procrastination, giving too much time to leisure activities (especially electronic games), and lengthy visiting on the telephone or via other communication devices.

Good time *managers use all their time*. They use "waiting time." If, for example, they find themselves waiting in a doctor's office, they pull out paper and a pencil and work on something that they had planned to do later, like writing a grocery list or memorizing a list of facts or perhaps grading papers. Ask someone who you see as a community person who "does a lot" about how they manage to do so much. You will find someone *that uses all her time*.

Dr. Covey, the great time expert, urges people to determine what to "do next" by determining whether the task is *urgent or not urgent, important or not important.* With that kind of analysis, of course you do first the task that is both urgent and important. With this kind of analysis, you can keep on track with your responsibilities within the timeframe you have.

Of course, we all have the same amount of time, only our responsibilities and our use of the time varies a great deal. It is always good manners not to waste the time of others, just as it is smart not to waste your own time.

A very productive teacher was interviewed about how she was able to accomplish so much. She said that she wastes no time; she explained:

- I work ahead on upcoming projects.
- When I get an assignment I start on it at once.
- I finish what I start before moving to something else.
- I prepare for tomorrow before I leave the office today.
- I do paperwork during waiting times, like in the doctor's office.
- When I am listening to a boring speaker, I just mentally shut him out and work on ideas for my next project.
- I enjoy what I do and I reward myself when I have reached a goal.
- I take care of my body.

TIME WASTERS

Time wasters are enemies to productivity. Here are common ones.

- lack of organization
- procrastination
- spending time with technology that is not work-related
- bad health
- lack of knowledge for specific tasks
- talking to others about things unrelated to work
- interruptions
- perfectionism
- lack of cooperation

BECOMING MORE PRODUCTIVE THROUGH SYNERGY

Adopt the attitude that "synergy" (the result of two or more people working together to solve problems and be more productive together than either can be alone) is important in your work life. With an attitude of cooperativeness and appreciation for the abilities of your colleagues, work to reach organizational goals. Practice the interpersonal skills you know to be effective so that you will be welcome on work teams and group projects.

MOVING UP THE CAREER LADDER

When you have chosen your career field, be the best you can be. For example, be the best benefits analyst or the best banker or the best teacher that you can be! Once you are recognized for excellence at work, you will be tapped for a higher-level position. Here are some ways that you can be your very best.

- Work hard; nothing promotes success like persistence.
- Keep learning; be current in your field, in the latest technologies, and in community and world events.
- Get more training in your field.
- Practice a positive approach to work.
- Participate in professional organizations.
- Make a plan to reach your professional goals.
- Set your sights on your next career step and work toward it.
- Constantly work on your interpersonal skills.

Here are the notes from an interview with a young teacher who was recently promoted to school principal. The interviewer asked how she had moved up the career ladder so quickly. The new principal answered:

- I worked diligently to be a good teacher.
- I took evening and online classes to get a Principal's Certificate.
- I got to know people outside my own building by participating in the largest educator's organization in town.
- I followed all the school policies and rules with a positive attitude.

- My students' scores on state tests were exceptionally high.
- I tried to be loyal at all times to my students, my coworkers, and my school.
- I joined the Chamber of Commerce and participated in community events as I had time.

MOVING ON TO MOVE UP

When the careers of many people are viewed from a long-term perspective, it appears that people who are willing to move physically whenever a new opportunity becomes available are the ones who reach the top of the career ladder. Additionally, the young people who move often are usually those who reach great heights in their careers.

For a two-career family, the physical moves become a problem when one has an opportunity for a new and better position and the other one in the couple does not have such an opportunity. That problem is best solved if the couple discusses such a possibility before they marry; however, married couples solve the problem in a variety of ways. For example, a teacher who has an opportunity to become a principal while her husband does not have an opportunity for moving may choose to have a weekend marriage or a long-distance marriage. And, in the interest of fairness, some couples decide to alternate opportunities for promotion. In other words, this year, if one gets a better post, next year they concentrate on the advancement of the other one.

REMEMBER:

1. Set your goals for the next step in your career.
2. Keep learning and developing career-related skills.
3. Practice habits that lead to promotion.
4. When you are ready for the next step and there is a job opening that is right for you, apply for it with confidence!

References

Baldridge, L. *Letitia Baldridge's Complete Guide to the New Manners for the '90s*. New York: Rawson Associates, 1990.

Bogan, C. "An Insider's Guide to Social Etiquette." Available at www.chrisbrogan.com/socialmediaetiquette. Retrieved December 2, 2011.

Burleson, D. *Business Etiquette for Professionals*. Available at www.dba-oracle.com/consultant_etiquette_manners.htm. Retrieved October 31, 2011.

Campbell, S., and D. Taylor. "Professionalism in the Workplace." Available at http://hosting.caes.uga.edu/2008csrees/pdfs/S54-Workplace%20Professionalism.pdf. Retrieved February 7, 2012.

Couch, C., G. Felstehausen, and P. Hallman. *Skills for Life*. Minneapolis/St. Paul: West Publishing Company, 1997.

Covey, S. *First Things First*. New York: Simon & Schuster, 1994.

———. *Seven Habits of Highly Effective People*. New York. Simon & Schuster, 1990.

Craig, B. *Don't Slurp Your Soup*. New Brighton, MN: New Brighton Publications, 1991.

Feinberg, J. "World—Create." Available at http://wordle.net/create. Retrieved February 7, 2012.

Grant-Sokolosky, V. *Corporate Protocol*. Tulsa, OK: Honor, 1986.

Hallman, P. *Creating a Positive Self-Image*. Lanham, MD: Scarecrow Education, 1994.

———. Interview with B. Schneider on sportsmanship. November 2012.

———. Interview with B. Spurrier and D. Spurrier on social media in large businesses. December 20, 2011.

———. Interview with C. Hardy on university admissions, Stephen F. Austin State University. August 8, 2011.

———. Interview with M. Spurrier on high school athletics. August 1, 2011.

———. Interview with R. Underwood on professionalism. February 1, 2012.

———. Interview with university students studying methods of teaching at Stephen F. Austin State University, Nacogdoches, Texas, 2004.

———. Lectures from Human Sciences 350 (Professionalism). Stephen F. Austin State University, 2005.

Hallman, P., and L. Johnson. *Building a Professional Life.* Albany, NY: Delmar, 1992.

Hubbard, E. Quote available at www.brungquote.com/quotes/quotes/e/elbert hubb. Retrieved May 6, 2012.

Johnson, L. Comments to her granddaughters, Rebecca Johnson, Patsy Johnson, and Peggy Burns. Miller Grove, Texas, 1952.

Kennedy, L. *Essential Business Etiquette.* Corpus Christi, TX: Palmetto Publishing, 1997.

Kenner, J., R. Underwood, and S. McCune. "Principal's Perception of Teaching Effectiveness as Defined by Teacher Dress." *Journal of Family and Consumer Sciences Education* 20, no. 2 (Fall/Winter 2002). Available at www.natefacs.org/JFCSE/v20no2/v20no2abstractUnderwood.pdf. Retrieved April 14, 2012.

Mitchell, N. "The Etiquette Advocate." Available at www.etiquetteadvocate.com. Retrieved October 21, 2011.

Mix, T. Thursday, (February 2, 2012). Nacogdoches, Texas: *Opinions, College Dress Codes.* The Pine Log, Stephen F. Austin State University Newspaper.

Parry, J. "New Friends and Old Friends" in *The Best Loved Poems of the American People.* New York: Garden City Books, 1936.

Post, E. *Emily Post's Etiquette.* New York: Funk & Wagnall, 1984.

Ramsey, L. *Top 12 Rules of Social Media Etiquette.* Available at www.businessknowhow.com/internet/socialmediaetiquette.htm. Retrieved April 14, 2012.

"Sportsmanship." Wikipedia. Available at http://en.wikipedia.org/wiki/Sportsmanship. Retrieved April 14, 2011.

Wilcox, E. "You Never Can Tell" *The Best Loved Poems of the American People.* New York: Garden City Books, 1936.

About the Author

Patsy Johnson Hallman, Ph.D., is professor emeritus and retired dean, College of Education, Stephen F. Austin State University, Nacogdoches, Texas. In addition to teaching at all levels, K–16, she has authored and coauthored several books. Her professional interests, as leader, teacher, professor, and writer have always centered on teachers and teaching.

Dr. Hallman places high priority on her family: husband Dr. Leon Hallman, children, grandchildren, and brothers. Among her retirement interests are family, volunteering within the community, reading, writing, speaking, and gardening.

Among her many honors are "Leader of the Year" among Texas Deans of Colleges of Education, "Distinguished Professor" at her university, and "Citizen of the Year" in her community.

CPSIA information can be obtained at www.ICGtesting.com
Printed in the USA
BVOW021310170612

292836BV00002B/6/P